"HEARTBREAK RIDGE— WITHOUT QUESTION THE MOST SAVAGE SINGLE ACTION OF THE KOREAN WAR."

—*Indianapolis Star*, November 11, 1951

WARRIORS OF THE HILL

PFC. GERALD UNDERWOOD: Against a storm of bullets the private from Missouri crawled out into the open. A few yards from the enemy bunker, he threw his grenades, then stood up and gunned down the fleeing enemy troops . . .

BRIGADIER GENERAL THOMAS DE SHAZO: The acting commanding general believed his men could overcome enemy resistance in a day. When the battle reports came back to him, he said, "My reputation is at stake. Go take that damn hill."

LIEUTENANT GENERAL RALPH MONCLAR: The commander of the French forces in Korea looked like Spencer Tracy and fought like the devil. A protégé of De Gaulle, he called the battle "equal to Verdun," and devised a strategy for victory . . .

COLONEL JAMES ADAMS: His men called him "Skinny Adams" and would follow him into any fight. But after he met the North Koreans on Heartbreak Ridge, he told his superiors: "To continue as we have been doing is suicide."

PRIVATE CARL KLEINPETER: He and his cousin, Olen, had both been assigned to the Second "Indianhead" Division. At the front line they would be separated—and both would see the blood and horror, and be wounded in the fight . . .

CAPTAIN JAMES DICK: He had volunteered for an infantry division in order to see more combat. On September 23 he led two courageous assaults of Hill 931 as a hailstorm of grenades poured down. Hit in the leg, he refused to be evacuated until he led Company A to the top . . .

HEARTBREAK RIDGE

KOREA, 1951

Arned L. Hinshaw

POCKET BOOKS

New York   London   Toronto   Sydney   Tokyo   Singapore

POCKET BOOKS, a division of Simon & Schuster Inc.
1230 Avenue of the Americas, New York, NY 10020

Copyright © 1989 by Arned Lee Hinshaw

ISBN: 0-671-70425-7

First Pocket Books printing October 1990

10 9 8 7 6 5 4 3 2 1

POCKET and colophon are registered trademarks of
Simon & Schuster Inc.

Cover photo courtesy of Harry Kane & Associates

Printed in the U.S.A.

*To the men and women of all nationalities
who helped ensure the free existence
of the Republic of Korea*

Contents

Contents

Maps

~~~~~~~~

Abbreviations

~~~~~~~~

ADC	assistant division commander
ASP	ammunition supply point
BAR	Browning automatic rifle
BOQ	bachelor officer quarters
Brig. Gen.	brigadier general
C.A.	Heavy Weapons Company (French Battalion)
Capt.	captain
CCF	Chinese communist forces
CINCFE	commander-in-chief, Far East
CINCUNC	commander-in-chief, United Nations command

CO	commanding officer
Col.	colonel
comdr.	commander
CP	command post
Cpl.	corporal
EM	enlisted man
ExO	executive officer
FA	field artillery
G-1	personnel section of divisional or higher staff
G-2	intelligence section of divisional or higher staff
G-3	operations and training section of divisional or higher staff
G-4	logistics section of divisional or higher staff
ISF	Ivanhoe Security Force
KIA	killed in action
LD	line of departure
Lt. Col.	lieutenant colonel
Lt. Gen.	lieutenant general
Maj.	major
Maj. Gen.	major general
MASH	mobile army surgical hospital
MIA	missing in action
MP	military police
M. Sgt.	master sergeant
N.K.	North Korean
O.C.S.	officers candidate school
Pfc.	private first class

Abbreviations

POW	prisoner-of-war
Pvt.	private
RCT	regimental combat team
ROK	Republic of Korea
ROTC	reserve officer training corps
Sfc.	sergeant first class
Sous-Lt.	sous lieutenant (French)
Sqd. Ldr.	squad leader
WIA	wounded in action
1st Lt.	first lieutenant
2nd Lt.	second lieutenant

Foreword

This stirring historical account centering on Heartbreak Ridge puts that costly battle in its proper perspective in a struggle for independence for a nation that the United States had brought into being, and that it had an ineluctable responsiblity to support, not vicariously, but in our own direct defense.

I feel there is little I can add to so well researched and detailed an addition to the history of the Korean War.

> M. B. Ridgway
> General, United States Army, Retired

Acknowledgments

~~~~~~

Preparing acknowledgments is probably the most difficult aspect of authoring a book. So many contribute so much in many different ways before the finished product is achieved. Some that should be mentioned will be left out just as not all the heroes of a battle can be included in the story's telling. Unable to place any priority on their help, I will simply thank in chronological order my valued contributors.

First, Maj. Gen. Haydon L. Boatner, now deceased, provided the inspiration way back in 1954 when the author served as a young lieutenant on that general's staff. General Boatner, the assistant division commander of the Second Infantry Division on Heartbreak Ridge, came to Fort Benning, Georgia, to command the Third Infantry Division. He presented a tough exterior but talked openly of the personal heartbreak he felt in sending, time and time again, good men to their certain death.

An army assignment over 30 years later in Washington, D.C., provided the author with the opportunity to research extensively battle reports and other official documents at the National Archives, Suitland, Maryland. But personal interviews were needed to make the story come alive.

Rudy Avila, President of the Twenty-third Infantry Korean War Branch, a unique veterans' organization, responded immediately to an inquiry and invited the author to their next meeting in Des Moines, Iowa. Roy Mogged contacted Guy Robinson, who in turn provided names, pictures, and maps and served as a central clearing point for information.

Interviews were conducted in Des Moines, in Covington, Louisiana, in Beaufort, South Carolina, in San Francisco, in Battle Creek, Michigan, in Washington, D.C., and in Paris, France. Some interviews took place at unusual locations and under varied circumstances: Jim Dick in his hospital room at Walter Reed Army Hospital; Guy Robinson on the deck of a boat on the Potomac River; Maj. Gen. Richard Kotite at the Capital Yacht Club in Washington, D.C.; Xavier Moissinac-Massénat on a bus to Rheims, France; and Joe Melton in a Paris hotel until well past midnight, although he was to leave on a trip early the next morning to Normandy. While the author was talking with General and Mrs. Mildren in their home on Lady's Island, South Carolina, radio broadcasts were every few minutes predicting that hurricane Diana would strike the area momentarily. The general nonchalantly commented that it was not unusual for high waters to flood their grounds.

Monsieur Hubert Segond gave personal attention to

arrangements for the author to attend a meeting of French veterans in Paris. On a train from Frankfurt to Paris, Capt. Stephen W. Smith, then in the Judge Advocate Corps of the United States Army, introduced himself and volunteered an entire day of his time in Paris to help the author make appointments and to serve as an interpreter. He later translated, from the French, Oliver Le Mire's account of Heartbreak Ridge.

The French were most gracious. Generals Barthélémy and de Cockborne entertained the author, Barthélémy at the Cercle National de l'Armée in Paris and de Cockborne at his chateau at Ervy-le-Chatel. A visit to Ervy-le-Chatel is like taking a walk back in time to medieval France.

Serge Bererd accompanied the author on the metro to Fort D'Ivry, where the French army photographic services are located, to view a film of Heartbreak Ridge. He later read those portions of the manuscript about the French role and made useful corrections. Another translator, Larry Potemra at the Gangplank Marina, Washington, D.C., rendered valuable assistance. Dr. Rodney P. Carlisle, Professor of History, Rutgers University, and a naval military historian, *critically* reviewed a draft of the manuscript. His help was invaluable.

Gen. Matthew B. Ridgway read a draft of the manuscript, made some interesting and important corrections, and wrote the book's Foreword. That short statement is of itself historically significant, for it reveals that after 35 years the supreme commander unswervingly believes in the rightness of our cause. General Ridgway replaced General of the Army Douglas MacArthur in command in Tokyo and later replaced General of the Army Dwight Eisenhower as Supreme Commander, Allied Powers in Europe. A fitting recognition of Matthew Ridgway's renowned and dedicated service would be for his country to promote him, also, to five-star rank.

I shall be forever grateful to Emory S. Adams, Jr., for sending the manuscript to General Ridgway.

I thank my son, Ned, for his help in preparing the maps and photographs. Only with the help and constant encouragement of my wife, Virginia, was this work accomplished. She typed and retyped for hours at a time, producing a beautiful manuscript from my scribblings.

Introduction

~~~~~~~

Let there be no mistake about it. The Korean War was a clear win for the United States and the United Nations.[1] Not stated in clear terms, the sole war aim of the democracies was to prevent the Republic of Korea from falling under communist domination. This they achieved. South Korea remained free to pursue its independent destiny for over 35 years after North Korean and Chinese aggression intended it to become yet another country imprisoned behind the iron curtain.

North Korea and China failed miserably to achieve

their war aims, however. China's involvement in Korea cost it heavily: Resources were drained severely, setting back social and economic programs many years for mainland China. It possibly replaced aggression that would have been directed against Formosa.

Today South Korea has been transformed from a primarily agricultural country to one of significant industrialization. Militarily strong, it stands as a strategic bulwark against Asian communism. Not only does the Republic of Korea's army stand ready to fight again if needed in defense of its homeland, it has also made significant contributions in Southeast Asia by sending some 50,000 men to help counter communism there. The Korean soldiers in Vietnam gave an account of themselves equal to that given by the soldiers who had come to aid them in their own hour of need from the British Commonwealth, France, Greece, Turkey, the Netherlands, and many other nations.

Peace now reigns in South Korea. As this is being written, representatives of nations from all over the globe are gathering there for the summer Olympics. In a spirit of unity and friendly rivalry some of the world's finest young women and men compete in athletic events enjoyed by millions. This result was achieved only through the effort of a successful United Nations.

Any suggestion that the Korean War was a "draw" is simply untrue. Who but MacArthur envisioned a conquest and occupation of North Korea? Certainly not the president of the United States. Harry

Truman's goals were to defend South Korea—and to avoid nuclear war.

At the end of the Korean War, a sensibly defensible line replaced the phantom 38th parallel as a demarcation between North and South Korea. The Second U.S. Division (with attached French and Netherlands Battalions), in taking Heartbreak Ridge, secured an important segment of that line. This book is the story of that bloody battle, the day-to-day engagements of platoons, companies, battalions, and regiments, and the face-to-face fighting with the enemy as experienced by the individual combat soldier.

An operation to take a complex of rugged hills, initially expected to be completed in one day, continued for a full month of bitter sacrifice as more and more troops from both sides were thrown into the struggle to replace an unprecedented number of killed and wounded. The reader will ask: How did such a gross miscalculation occur? Did the military planners underestimate the strength or the determination of the enemy force? Were the U.S. commanders misled about the enemy's fortifications? Did they use the wrong strategy in their many attempts to take the ridgeline? Was friendly fire support adequate?

The bravery, raw courage, and determination of the men who stood face to face against the enemy, even engaging in fist fights with him, are clear. Any judgment about the performance of the top commanders is left to the reader.

In telling this story the author has drawn from almost all the books about the Korean War available today, the official U.S. archives and histories of the war, and, most importantly, from personal interviews with many of the battle's surviving participants, both U.S. and French, four-star generals to privates (see Acknowledgments).

The U.S. men who fought for, and who died for, the continued freedom of that once obscure Asian country and the containment of communism were a breed unique to their times. The 1950s were a bridge between the exaggerated sentimentality of the 1940s and the cold cynicism of the 1960s and 1970s. The Korean War soldier was akin to his G.I. brother of World War II in his loyalty, obedience, and dedication to duty. Indeed, many of the troops in Korea had themselves fought in earlier battles in the Pacific and in Europe.

English historian Michael Langley has said that the Korean War "for some strange reason, is already passing into military oblivion."[2] There are indications that as a military subject it is emerging from a temporary eclipse, and we are to see more and more written about the Korean War.

Several new publications have appeared in just the last few years.[3] In fact, in the course of research for this book, the author has found that others with a like interest in the Korean War have works in progress.

PART
I

FIRST PHASE

1

A Naked Mountain

> Since the beginning of the war, the terrain has become
> more and more arduous, more and more elevated, more
> and more compact.
>
> *Major Le Mire,*
> *Deputy Commander, French Battalion[1]*

An early fall swept deceptively mild along Korea's
38th parallel. After a summer of hard fighting, the
Second U.S. Division moved to positions from where
they saw before them a dark mass of rock and rubble
soon to be known as Heartbreak Ridge. Looming
3,000 feet into the gray skies, it menaced the barren
landscape like a foreboding landlocked iceberg. Understandably, the men of the Second "Indianhead"

Division might ask, "Of what possible worth is this naked mountain to me—to my country?"

One who did not ask the question was Pvt. Carl Kleinpeter, an ammo bearer attached to E "Easy" Company, Twenty-third Infantry Regiment. His sergeant told his comrades and him, "Take that hill and you will be given a rest."

God knows, they needed a rest. Through summer's heat, through drenching rains pouring down upon them in the afternoons, every day since disembarking from the smoke-filled troop train that had carried Carl and his cousin, Olen Kleinpeter, northward from Pusan, he lugged two boxes of ammo, each one weighing 40 pounds, as well as his M-1 rifle and battlepack stashed with C-rations and shelter half. His heavy load pulled and strained at his muscles, making them ache in a way his work when growing up on a Louisiana farm had never done.

Olen and Carl Kleinpeter had grown up together in the parish of East Baton Rouge, Louisiana—sugar cane country. Olen was the oldest by two years and ten months. Neither of them had been old enough for World War II, but when the Korean War came along they were drafted at the same time into the United States Army.

Although in September 1951 Carl would turn 21—an important milestone in anyone's life—that month, especially one day in that month, would be fateful for Olen as well as for Carl.

When the Kleinpeter cousins got off the train, they learned for the first time to which division they were assigned. There was no formal announcement; they were just unceremoniously handed a large shield-shaped shoulder patch, black with a white star and an Indian's head, adorned by a chief's full-feathered battle bonnet. Then they were given a little kit with needle and thread and told to sew the patch onto their fatigues.

The Second Division was already heavily engaged. There was the Punchbowl, and at the end of August, Bloody Ridge, and now Heartbreak Ridge.

The main ridgeline ran north to south for about seven miles. It was made up of three principal peaks: Hill 894 at the southern terminus commanded the approach from Bloody Ridge, three miles to the south. Thirteen hundred yards to the north of Hill 894 rose the highest peak of the three, Hill 931. Twenty-one hundred yards to the north of Hill 931 stood a needle-like projection, Hill 851 (see Maps 1 and 2).[2] These distances were well within the range of infantry weapons, and thus the North Korean defenders could lay down supporting fires from one hill to the other.

On either side of the ridgeline and parallel to it lay a valley. The one to the east got its name from the village of Satae-ri, located to the north. An unimproved road and a narrow stream, the Sochon, traversed this valley. Although shallow, the stream was not readily crossed by either wheeled or tracked vehicles, for smooth rocks filled its bed and did not allow for easy traction.

Similarly the valley to the west, named for Mundung-ni Village to the north, was cut through by

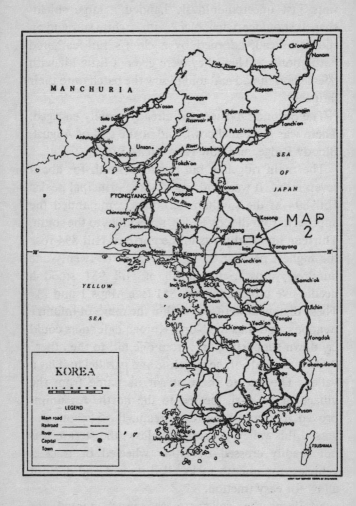

map 1
Korea with inset map of the Punchbowl and Heartbreak Ridge areas

the Suip-chon. Its accompanying road was even more impassable than that in the Satae-ri Valley because of large boulders encroaching upon its narrow path.

Extending west to east and east to west from the north-south ridgeline—Hills 894, 931, and 851—were many spurs that ran down into the Satae-ri and Mundung-ni valleys. One description likened the spurs to "the spinal column of a fish, with hundreds of vertebrae."[3]

But what the men of Second Division saw was just the tip of the iceberg.

The enemy had built elaborate fortifications on

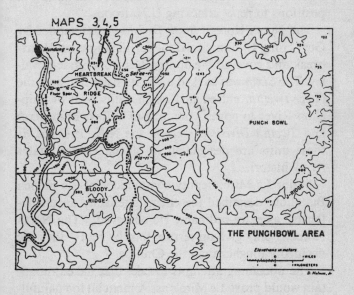

Map 2
The Punchbowl area with inset map of Heartbreak Ridge

11

Heartbreak Ridge. Mostly on the reverse or western slope facing Mundung-ni Valley, they had dug deep bunkers covered over with timbers, then hardened on top by dirt and rocks. So strong were they that one of these bunkers could resist a direct hit by a 105-mm howitzer shell, or anything less than a direct hit by a 250-pound bomb in an air strike. They were also well camouflaged.

There were enough bunkers to protect hundreds of men. Located only 25–30 yards from the topographical crest of the ridge, enemy troops could remain safely inside until preparatory artillery fires were lifted, then run to their many prepared machine-gun positions to repel attacking U.N. troops.

The North Korean *Sixth Division,* commanded by Gen. Hong Nim, manned the fortifications on Heartbreak and covered the approaches from Satae-ri Valley. The *Sixth* was backed up by its sister division, the N.K. *Twelfth,* entrenched on the hills west of Suipchon River to cover Mundung-ni Valley. Both *Sixth* and *Twelfth Divisions* were in the N.K. *V Corps,* as these units are designated in official United States Army histories.[4]

Major Le Mire, deputy commander of the French Battalion, described the enemy's tenacity on the defensive as extra-ordinary. He observed, "The North Koreans only give up terrain foot by foot—they are decidedly tougher than the Chinese."[5]

The upcoming attempts to take that naked mountain would prove Le Mire's assessment all too painfully accurate. General Hong Nim and his well-trained infantry would stubbornly hold onto that ridgeline like a bulldog with a prized bone clenched between his teeth.

The terrain the North Koreans had chosen to defend gave the enemy yet another advantage: Reinforcement and resupply of forces was made easier by a more gentle slope on the western side.

Another who did not ask the question was Pfc. Guy Robinson from Normal, Illinois. He was now an assistant Browning automatic rifle (BAR) gunner in K "King" Company, Twenty-third Infantry Regiment. Guy, whose soft blue eyes and soft voice were indicative of his sensitive, perceptive nature, would quietly volunteer to help recover under hazardous conditions the body of a slain comrade, although he had already seen much of death.

Too much death, in fact. The first time was while moving up to Heartbreak Ridge in a column over a rocky trail along So-chon stream. Beside the trail he saw a dead body with one small shrapnel wound right in the temple area. It was the body of Quinn Reidy, who had come over to Korea with him on the same ship.

Guy's emotions upon seeing his dead friend were difficult, in later years, to describe. He experienced "a funny feeling," and a big lump formed in his throat. He wanted to cry. But he did not cry. He did not say a single word. Instead he just kept on moving with the column, fixing his eyes on the man in front. It was all he could do.

Others in Guy Robinson's squad—the First Squad, Third Platoon, K Company—besides Sq. Ldr. Willie

Shimabukuro were riflemen Cliff Karlson, Frank Madrid, and Al Terney and BAR gunners Delmar Burchett, John M. Seybert, Jr., and Al Seghetti.

Bud, as John Seybert was known, wrote home often, beginning his letters with "Dear Mom and all." He was one of six from Collinsville, Illinois, inducted in January 1951 and trained together with the Sixth Armored Division at Fort Leonard Wood, Missouri, before coming to Korea.

That had been three months before. One of their number had already been killed. Two, including Bud, had already been wounded. Luckily, though, Bud's injuries from a booby-trapped hand grenade had not been serious, and after a short stay in Osaka, Japan, he was returned to duty.

The beautiful weather of this fall season in Korea made Bud think of home and its fields of tall, golden Illinois corn. "These autumn days are making me homesick," he admitted in a letter to his family. "Believe this is the best part of the year."[6]

But here there was no corn. There was hardly anything growing at all, for what trees had once adorned the valleys had all been destroyed by massive artillery barrages raining heavy steel down upon them and cratering the ground all around them. Most had been blown clean away leaving ragged stumps, while the rest were split and splintered.

No hero, by his own account, Bud Seybert just pushed on line when he was told, firing his automatic rifle when told. He never wore his steel helmet after the first few days because its weight pressing down on his skull gave him a headache. A risky chance to take,

14

but Bud would go through Heartbreak without another scratch.

Yet Guy Robinson would never see the top of Heartbreak Ridge. Neither would Willie Shimabukuro, nor Al Terney. Nor would BAR gunner Al Seghetti, Guy's teammate and best friend.

Others were more fortunate. For all the front line evacuees who asked him enviously how he got such a plush job, Cpl. Frederick Dillon had a ready answer: "I got here the same way you did. I was wounded."

The circuitous journey that had brought Fred to the 629th Medical Clearing Company at Chunchon began back in May 1951 at Inje, where shrapnel from a 4.2-mm mortar had hit Fred in the cheek, shoulder, hip, and groin. He was evacuated in a C-47 to Pusan and finally to Osaka, Japan. A partial hearing loss from the round's loud explosion prevented his return to duty with a line company, and so he was reassigned to the medical unit.

Although he had never had any medical training (he had been drafted from Salom Springs, Arkansas, where he was an industrial arts teacher), Fred enjoyed his work. Here the men were quartered in squad tents, they ate prepared meals in a mess tent, and they took care of patients in hospital ward tents. The clearing company was by no means entirely out of danger, being located just 30 miles from the front lines, but their situation was far better than that of the troops on line.

Fred Dillon helped move the wounded about on litters as they came into the clearing company for triage, started IVs, drew blood, and even did some suturing. He liked working with the doctors, especially one black physician, a Lieutenant Fountain from Pennsylvania, who patiently taught him and the other on-the-job trainees.

Somewhat shorter than average height, Fred always seemed to wear a perpetual grin on his face. From his point of view of the world, everything could be tempered with a dash of humor. Once while clearing an area the bulldozers unearthed an old cemetery. Out of the rubble the men got hold of a skeleton, which they proceeded to wrap in blankets and lay on a litter. They then filled out a regulation medical tag listing as diagnoses a fractured skull, fractured left and right femurs, broken ribs, and for good measure, diarrhea. Rounding up a doctor, they told him, "We have just gotten a patient that you need to see right away."

Everyone got a hearty laugh. Macabre humor? Perhaps, but then the horrors of war can encourage macabre humor. A day would come soon when there would be no time for even an occasional practical joke, macabre or not. Everyone at the clearing company would be working around the clock as all the casualties from Heartbreak Ridge began arriving.

2

The First Year: War of Movement

Harry Truman was totally without what he called "that most enfeebling of emotions, regret."

Dean Acheson,
U.S. Secretary of State, 1949–53[1]

Harry Truman had every right to be satisfied with himself, and he was—immensely satisfied. When he became thirty-fourth president of the United States in April 1945 upon the sudden death of Franklin Delano Roosevelt, who was regarded with near godlike reverence, the man from Missouri was overwhelmed by the awesome responsibility thrust upon him and by his own feelings of inadequacy. All of this soon changed.

Harry Truman adopted the slogan "The Buck Stops Here."

Within the first few days of taking the highest office, he was faced with a momentous decision unequaled by that of any president before him. The time had come in the United States' greatest war to invade the home islands of a fanatical enemy. Perhaps a million U.S. lives would be lost.

But there was an alternative. A bomb using nuclear energy had been developed under such a cloak of super-secrecy that not even the vice president of the United States knew of its existence. With power equivalent to 20,000 tons of TNT, President Truman was now told, a single atomic bomb could produce untold destruction of life and property by its shock wave and flash heat.

The president was not told about *another* significant aspect of this instrument of destruction—that the atomic bomb also released radiation capable of causing widespread illness and death. Or further, that these lethal radiation effects would be long term. It could not be told because at that time the very scientists who had developed the nuclear weapon were unable to predict the full scope of this heretofore untested feature.

Harry Truman made his decision. The first atomic bomb dropped on Hiroshima at 8:16 A.M. on August 6, 1945.[2] Three days later the Soviet Union declared war on Japan. The Red Army moved into Manchuria in what was to be the final hours of this great conflict, for on August 14, just five days after two of its principal cities (Nagasaki was the second victim of a nuclear attack) had been devastated, the Nippon government surrendered unconditionally.

World War II was at an end, and the United States was at peace after nearly four years of war.

This sudden capitulation of Japan had its drawbacks, however. There had been no time to plan for an orderly surrender of the enemy's armies in the field. Particularly, across the Yellow Sea in Korea, which had been seized by Japan from Russia in the 1904–06 war, there were thousands of Japanese under arms.

Expediency dictated the solution: The United States could best take surrender of those forces in the south nearest Japan while the Soviets who had entered the war against Japan at the last moment readily accepted a conqueror's role in the north nearest Siberia. A line running across the anatomical waist of Korea, the 38th parallel, seemed as good as any to separate the two areas of control.

Although the war was over, it had precipitated conflicts worldwide that called for President Truman's attention. He moved decisively. For when communist guerrilla pressure increased in eastern Turkey and northern Greece, and Great Britain signaled its inability to continue support, effective aid was sent to these two countries in the form of the Truman Doctrine. To assist in rebuilding a wardevastated Europe, the U.S. government proposed the Marshall Plan, the seed that grew and blossomed into full economic recovery for that industrial continent.

The general elections in the United States came in the fall of 1948, and Harry Truman conducted an unprecedented one-man whistle-stop campaign, soundly beating his "unbeatable" opponent and win-ning his "political self-respect as a man and President."[3]

After it became apparent that the Soviet Union was not going to cooperate in forming a unified government for Korea, the United Nations held elections in the South, and as a result, Syngman Rhee was elected president. On January 1, 1949, the Republic of Korea was recognized by the United States. In the North, meanwhile, the Soviet Union created the People's Republic of Korea, thus setting the stage for future conflict. To deal with Soviet aggression in Europe, dramatized by a communist-led coup d'état that vanquished the Czechoslovak republic, the United States led in formulating the North Atlantic Treaty in April 1949.

Foreign affairs were far from any satisfactory resolution. But it now appeared that more likely there would be a chronic, long-term stand-off rather than immediate confrontation between the two super powers that had emerged—the United States and the Soviet Union. (The latter exploded its first nuclear device in September 1949.)

The U.S. economy continued expanding on an even plane to take care of housing and other needs of the many returning World War II veterans, and by mid-1950 Harry Truman, thirty-fourth president of the United States, had every right to believe his major crises, both personal and political, were behind him.

Saturday, June 24, was shaping up to be a lazy mid-summer's day. The *Washington Post* was forecasting a high near 90° and scattered afternoon thundershowers, the culmination of a long, dry hot spell. Washingtonians were being enticed to come to Lacy's downtown store or one of its five branches ("all 6 stores are air conditioned") to buy brand new televisions, "brand new 1950 models" for "as low as $18."[4]

There were other things to do, too: Go to the "cool" Low's Palace Theater and see Betty Hutton in *Annie Get Your Gun*—in technicolor, no less; or on this hot Saturday afternoon stay home, probably without air conditioning, and listen to baseball over the radio— the Washington Senators vs. the Cleveland Indians. That game was being played in Cleveland.

Official Washington was looking forward to getting out of the city for a restful weekend. Secretary of State Dean Acheson departed for Harewood Farm in Maryland, just 20 miles north of Washington, "very quiet and very secluded."[5] He planned to do some gardening.[6]

President Truman chafed at the thought of giving a speech in Baltimore for dedication of the new $15 million Friendship International Airport. Politically wise, he gave the speech and then reboarded the *Independence,* the four-engine (2,500 hp) presidential Douglas DC-6 with a cruising speed of 316 miles per hour. (Militarily procured as a C-118, it had been converted for the commander-in-chief's special needs.) His mind was preoccupied with the family farm in Grandview, Missouri: The farmhouse needed a new roof, and some fences needed building.

White House press secretary Charles Ross passed the word. "He will spend the entire weekend at his home in Independence and return to Washington

Monday afternoon." Emphasizing the personal nature of the trip, Ross announced, "He will make no public appearances and no speeches. He just wants to go home and sit quietly on the back porch for a little rest."[7]

Upon landing in Kansas City at two P.M. after a plane ride without "a bump in it," according to his own description, Truman was met by his sister, Mary Jane Truman, and by friends. He then motored for 30 minutes without motorcade escort the 12 miles to Independence, where his wife, Bess, was waiting at their two-story Victorian house on Delaware Street. She was spending the summer there, for she didn't care that much for Washington and she had not met him in Kansas City because it was just too hot. Some neighbors had gathered outside the house, and the president, wearing a light-colored, double-breasted suit, white straw hat, and carrying his cane, greeted them warmly: "I just came out to see the folks."[8]

The news reporters were pleased to hear him add that he would not be taking his early morning walk the next day. These famous Truman walks allowed them an informal interview unlike that with any previous chief executive. Often they had elicited some newsworthy statements from the frank-speaking president. But this particularly quiet weekend certainly did not offer anything promising. They, too, looked forward to a few leisurely days.

With dinner over, Bess, daughter Margaret, who had joined them, and Truman retired to the small library. It was now eight P.M., Central Standard Time.

The telephone rang. Truman answered it.

"Mr. President," he heard Dean Acheson's voice on the other end saying, "I have very serious news. The North Koreans have invaded South Korea."[9]

The president offered to return to Washington at once, but his secretary of state dissuaded him against a hazardous night flight. Instead, he left Kansas City on the *Independence* the next day, exactly 24 hours after he had arrived home.

Once again, President Truman acted swiftly and decisively. He ordered the United States Air Force and Navy "to give to the Korean Government troops cover and support."[10] This was in response to a call by the UN Security Council for North Korea to cease hostilities and withdraw its armed forces to the 38th parallel and for "all member nations to render every assistance to the United Nations in execution of this resolution." The resolution, adopted during a Sunday afternoon meeting of the council at the time the president was flying back to Washington, was passed without a single negative vote. Yugoslavia abstained, however, and the Soviet representative Joseph Malik, who most assuredly would have cast a veto, was boycotting the council ostensibly because of Nationalist China's presence.[11]

Almost from the very moment he had received the news of hostilities, Truman became obsessed with the thought of preventing World War III, which most likely would mean use of nuclear weapons. Although he never had any regret about his actions, he alone had borne the responsibility for all the misery wrought that one and only time an atomic bomb had been used in warfare. He was determined it would not happen again.

This obsession colored all of President Truman's subsequent decisions.

On the morning of June 29 General Douglas MacArthur, then supreme commander in Tokyo, boarded the *Bataan*. He flew through gray overcast skies to Suwon, 20 miles south of Seoul, the South Korean capital, which was at that very moment under heavy enemy attack.

As he had often done before in World Wars I and II, MacArthur, in contemptuous disregard for his own safety, raced in a jeep straight toward the forward-most action, which at this time was on the Han River. From the top of a little hill he watched for an hour, "streaming by both sides of the hill—the retreating, panting columns of disorganized troops" and refugees "[c]logging all the roads in a writhing, dust-shrouded mass of humanity."[12]

For the next several weeks this mass of disorganized troops and refugees heading southward grew like a rolling snowball in size and momentum. Those limited military forces[13] that the United States was able to throw into the path of the onrushing North Koreans did not appreciably slow their southward movement.

There was no stopping until reaching the Pusan perimeter. As his forces were about to be pushed into the sea, General Walker, the Eighth Army commander, ordered, "There will be no retreating, withdrawal, readjustment of lines, or whatever you call it."[14] A defense line around the perimeter was then established, and the retreat ended.[15]

The established command ran from General of the Army Douglas MacArthur, the commander-in-chief, Far East (CINCFE), and more recently designated the commander-in-chief, United Nations Command (CINCUNC), to Gen. Walton H. Walker, Eighth Army commander, with headquarters at Taegu, just inside the northwest corner of the perimeter.[16] In Pusan perimeter, under General Walker, were all the forces assembled through auspices of the United Nations. Together with the South Koreans, a large proportion of whom were labor units, the force totaled about 180,000 by the end of the summer of 1950.[17]

The North Korean advance was finally halted on September 10, 1950.[18] Just five days later MacArthur executed his masterful plan for an amphibious landing at Inchon Harbor, 18 miles west of Seoul. In an overwhelmingly successful maneuver, the U.S. X Corps, principally made up of the First Marine Division and the Seventh Infantry Division, was put ashore. Once the beachhead was secured, Lt. Gen. Edward M. Almond, the X Corps commander, assumed responsibility for future operations.[19]

With lines of communication disrupted and rear threatened, the enemy made a general withdrawal from Pusan perimeter.[20] The Eighth Army was able to break out and on September 26 joined forces with X Corps. Seoul was recaptured.

The 38th parallel was crossed in October as victorious U.N. forces swept on across North Korea, with its lead elements on November 21 reaching the Yalu River, which marked the boundary between that country and Manchuria, a part of communist China.

It was now that Chinese "volunteers," 200,000 strong, poured across the border, striking hard at the Eighth Army's right flank. MacArthur observed, "We face an entirely new war."[21] That new war saw the U.N. troops reeling back in the face of vastly superior numbers. Their winter retreat in subzero temperatures has been likened to the agonizing retreats from Moscow through snow and freezing weather of Napoleon's and Hitler's armies.[22]

While trying to stem the Asian tide that was lashing with hurricane force against his army, General Walker was killed in a jeep accident the day before Christmas Eve. Lt. Gen. Matthew B. Ridgway, intimately familiar with current Korean operations by reason of his Department of Army assignment as deputy chief of staff for operations and administration, was MacArthur's choice to become the new Eighth Army commander. Within 24 hours Ridgway was on his way to Tokyo. So swift was his departure that he forgot to pack the one thing he needed most—his track flannels that had kept him warm in the Ardennes seven years before.[23]

The North Koreans, now with Chinese help, crossed the 38th parallel on New Year's Eve for their second invasion of South Korea in six months. While a pull back into another Pusan perimeter, or even complete evacuation through Pusan Harbor, was seriously considered and detailed planning undertaken, this time a line was stabilized across the peninsula about 35 miles south of Seoul.[24]

From this line a U.N. counteroffensive was launched on January 25, 1951. Successive advances carried them back toward the 38th parallel, and Seoul was again in friendly hands by March 18. At the end of the month South Korea was cleared of all organized enemy forces. By April 9, UN troops reached the Kansas line, which ran from the junction of the Han and Imjin rivers northward and eastward to Yanyang.[25]

Now Harry Truman faced his third greatest decision, if dropping the atomic bomb on Hiroshima and Nagasaki be considered his first, and his decision to commit ground troops into Korea, his second. Public pronouncements by General MacArthur about Truman's imposed restrictions on the conduct of the war were causing the president two major concerns: His delicately stacked diplomatic house might be upset, resulting in the war's spread; and it appeared to him that the authority of the presidency over the military was being challenged.

He had probably already made up his mind to remove MacArthur from direct involvement with Korea, but he sought the advice of his senior officials nonetheless. They recommended MacArthur's immediate dismissal in the light of what they believed to be clear standing orders prohibiting diplomatic or political statements by military commanders. No face-saving alternative for the proud MacArthur was suggested by his military peers.

27

Whatever harm upon troop morale might have resulted from their supreme commander's abrupt dismissal was greatly minimized by selecting Ridgway as his successor. As commander of the Eighth Army the popular general, who always carried a hand grenade fastened to a paratrooper jump harness that he wore, had more than proved his leadership abilities. Although not a household name like many other World War II generals, Ridgway emerges as one of the United States Army's more brilliant and effective commanders. With this assessment there is agreement from privates and generals alike.

Lt. Gen. James A. Van Fleet was named to replace Ridgway as Eighth Army commander. Van Fleet arrived in Korea just eight days before the Chinese counter-counteroffensive began, on April 22. In that encounter the Eighth Army was forced back an average of 35 miles along the front, but the enemy offensive then fizzled out.[26]

Van Fleet then launched an attack along the entire front and at the end of May was almost back to Line Kansas.[27] Numerous enemy casualties were inflicted, and the Chinese experienced severe supply problems. By mid-June, the Eighth Army reached Line Kansas-Wyoming.[28] Line Wyoming extended out from Line Kansas in the center sector, touching the base of the Iron Triangle, which was formed with Pyonggang at its apex, Chorwon at the southwest angle, and Kumhwo at the southeast angle. This triangle was an important area of enemy troop and supply concentration.[29]

Van Fleet believed the Iron Triangle to be the best line on which to maintain a defensive posture looking to a cease-fire. A cease-fire was still a long way off, but armistice negotiations got under way at the village of Kaesong on July 10. The war of movement was over: The static war would last twice as long.

3

The Static War: Assault on Heartbreak Ridge

Heartbreak. It is the harsh reality of a thick mountain chain, five kilometers long. . . .

Major Le Mire,
Deputy Commander, French Battalion[1]

In one important respect there is little difference between a war of movement and a static war: In the first, the fighting man is killed while his army is on the move; in the second, he dies in a more closely defined area. To him the results are the same: His maiming is just as disabling, his death just as final.

While armistice negotiations were going on at Kaesong, it was a natural tendency for the fighting man, for his loved ones back home, and for the politicians to think that offensive actions to take more ground (which just might be returned to the enemy at the conference table) were futile, and that any further expenditure of lives should be avoided. General Van Fleet, however, concluded, "I couldn't allow my forces to become soft and dormant."[2] He believed, also, that there were some areas where his defensive positions could be improved and that pressure was necessary to keep the enemy off balance and less likely to mount an offensive.

The commanding ridges rimming the Punchbowl were seized in August, and Bloody Ridge to the west was taken in early September. After that, Van Fleet relayed to Ridgway his desire to undertake a "tidying up" on his right flank during the remainder of September.[3]

This was terminology Ridgway had heard before. As XVIII Airborne Corps commander in the Ardennes in 1944, he was once visited by Field Marshall Montgomery, who instructed him to "tidy up" his lines.[4]

Ridgway approved. The order went out on September 8 from Van Fleet to Maj. Gen. Clovis E. Byers, who had replaced Almond as X Corps commander: Take the high ground north of Bloody Ridge.

Indianhead Division was the choice of X Corps to carry out this difficult mission. No one envisioned just how difficult the task would be, however. Indianhead, the Second U.S. Infantry Division, was a typical triangular division having three infantry regiments, the Ninth, the Twenty-third and the Thirty-eighth. But there was an innovation at this particular time, for each of the infantry regiments was designated a Regimental Combat Team (RCT), having been augmented. Battalions were added: the Thailand Battalion to the Ninth, the French Battalion to the Twenty-third, and the Netherlands Battalion to the Thirty-eighth. Even with additional strength, though, a single division has its limitations.

When the directive was received at division headquarters, a heated discussion erupted. The division artillery commander, Col. Edwin A. "Ted" Walker, highly respected by his colleagues as one of the Army's finest battlefield commanders and tacticians despite his unorthodox political views,[5] was explicit: the North Koreans would "fight like hell."[6]

Brigadier General de Shazo, acting division commander, thought otherwise.[7] He planned to use only the Twenty-third Regiment to assault the ridgeline formed by Hills 894, 931, and 851. Of the Second Division's other two regiments, the Ninth Infantry was to give only limited support while the Thirty-eighth was to be held in division reserve.

However, an array of artillery was planned to support the infantry in their attack. The Thirty-seventh Field Artillery under Col. Linton S. "Buster" Boatright was in direct support of the Twenty-third. Its 105-mm howitzers were positioned about three miles southeast of the principal ridgeline.

In general support were the Thirty-eighth Field Artillery, commanded by Lt. Col. Marvin W. Flora, with its 105-mm howitzers positioned along with those of the Thirty-seventh, and the 503d Field Artillery Battalion (nicknamed the Nickle-Oh-Trey) with its 155-mm howitzers located nine miles southeast of the ridgeline. The Nickle-Oh-Trey was commanded by Lt. Col. H. E. Osthues.

Also in general support was the Ninety-sixth Field Artillery's 155-mm howitzers located about seven miles south of the main ridgeline. Battery C of the 780th Field Artillery would be firing its eight-inch howitzers (with 200-pound projectiles) from positions near Yack'on-Ni, about 11 miles to the south.

Col. John M. Lynch's Ninth Infantry would give fire support to the Twenty-third and afterward make an attack on Hill 728 lying 2,000 yards to the west and a little south of Hill 894.

The predawn hours of Thursday, September 13, saw the first attack upon the hill mass that would rightfully earn its name—Heartbreak Ridge. The Twenty-third's Second and Third Battalions shared the dubious honor of this first attack.

The evening before, Brigadier General de Shazo, acting commanding general, Second Infantry Division, had given an optimistic report to his superior, General Byers, the X Corps commanding general: "We are prepared to run into some fighting, but once we get that ridge we are going to hold it."[8]

The weather for the operation was expected to be near perfect—clear and cool. Visability in the early morning hours would be reduced to two or three miles but quickly rising to ten miles or better. A minimum early morning temperature of 54°F would reach 78°F as the day wore on. There would be no precipitation.[9]

Third Battalion (3/23) left its assembly area just east of Pia-ri at 0545 and moved north to pass through B Company's positions on Hill 702, which First Battalion (1/23) had wrested from the N.K. *First Regiment, Sixth Division,* in bitter fighting just the day before. Second Battalion (2/23) was to follow, in the words of de Shazo, "right on its tail."[10]

Pfc. Guy Robinson, trudging behind Willie Shimabukuro, his squad leader in King Company's Third Platoon, crooked the thumb of his right hand under his rifle's sling to adjust it on his shoulder and then ran his hand across his clean-shaven face. He was remembering the chilling words his platoon leader, 1st Lt. Daniel "Bill" Williams had said to them just before they were alerted to move out. Standing in front of the platoon in his bright Corcoran boots (his father sent him a new pair every four months from Stoughton, Massachusetts), the hefty lieutenant had told them, "I want to make sure you guys shave before we leave in case you get hit in the face." They all just looked blankly at each other as if to say, "Oh, my God, this is it!"[11]

A tall, thin figure with an M-1 rifle cradled in his arms could be seen standing beside the trail watching their movement closely. It was Col. James Yeates Adams, regimental commander of the Twenty-third. Adams, a 1935 West Point graduate, towered an imposing six feet six inches. Among themselves his men called him, not disrespectfully, Skinny Adams.

From Hill 702 the column descended through the gray fog hanging over Satae-ri Valley to a point near Samtae-dong. This was their designated line of departure (LD).

Before crossing the LD, Maj. Gene Craven, Third

Battalion commander, called for preplanned artillery fires to soften up the enemy. Thousands of shells from the artillery's 105-mm, 155-mm, and eight-inch howitzers rumbled through the early morning thin, cool air, exploding on the enemy's positions. This thundering barrage continued for 45 minutes for as the attacking troops and their commanders would soon discover, the artillery's effect upon the hardened, nearly impregnable North Korean bunkers was almost nil. Only after they had finally captured these North Korean bunkers would the U.S. troops learn just how sturdily they were constructed.

Third Battalion's L "Love" Company took the lead, jumping off at 0830, followed by I "Item" Company with K "King" Company behind Item. Initially they met no enemy resistance, although some enemy troops could be seen near Hill 841.

Twenty-third's mission did not seem all that difficult. The plan was this: Upon reaching the designated spur that extended eastward right down into Satae-ri Valley, which was to serve as their approach to the ridgeline, they were to turn west. Ascending the spur they would cut the ridgeline between the center hill (931) and the north hill (851). Third Battalion (3/23) would then turn north and secure Hill 851 while second Battalion (2/23) attacked down the ridgeline to take Hills 931 and 894 (see Map 3).

As the column moved along at route step, another Third Platoon, First Squad, man was engrossed in thought. Rifleman Al Terney began to rethink his decision to come to Korea. He liked his platoon mates, especially Al Seghetti from Peoria, Illinois, with whom he had become close friends, and Al Alward, the platoon radio operator, who would spend his evenings reading and writing letters for one illiterate man in their company. But Terney had had a relatively easy warehouseman's job in the 595th Engineer Company on Okinawa before volunteering for Korea.

At seventeen he had enlisted in the army for adventure—he wanted to see Alaska. He got his stint in Alaska and then arranged an assignment on Okinawa with his twin brother, John Terney, Jr., who had followed him into the army. With a war going on in Korea, the twin brothers, still "young and foolish," figured that was the place to be and were both eager to go. But their personnel officer said only one could go, applying a rule established in World War II after many painful experiences of brothers assigned to the same unit or to the same ship being killed simultaneously.

Al had been the one chosen to go. Now here he was as much in the war as he could be—and "it didn't seem so great after all."[12]

As Al's platoon approached the eastward-extending spur, the enemy began pouring heavy small arms and automatic weapons fire into their ranks. The enemy fire was coming from Hill 656 to the north, and from the west off the ridgeline between 931 and 851. Because of its unique position, projecting right down into Satae-ri Valley, Hill 656 was nicknamed the Watchdog.

One platoon of Item Company was placed in position to fire on Hill 656 and support the attack by Love and Item Companies. Soon Item was stopped by automatic weapons fire from the well-constructed enemy bunkers on 851. Incoming mortar fire from Hill 841 crashed down upon them.

Mortar rounds also began landing on King Company. The men in the column fell off on either side of the narrow, less than ten foot wide, trail. Guy Robinson saw that Willie Shimabukuro was hit. A piece of shrapnel had gone clean through his thigh.

Everyone crouched down however possible for some protection from the exploding rounds. When Guy next looked up at his squad leader, he expected to see him grimacing with pain. Instead Willie looked happy as he started limping back down the trail saying repeatedly, "I'm going home, I'm going home."

More mortars came in. Al Terney felt a sharp sting in the back of his right thigh, where he thought a flying stone had struck him. Running his hand down his leg, he found it covered with warm blood. He took off his web belt and wrapped it tightly around his thigh above the bleeding wound, as he had been taught he should do. Then hobbling down the trail as best he could, without assistance, he stumbled into some medics, who put him on a litter. Later he would be returned to K Company, but not until after Heartbreak.

In just these first hours of the move to attack, King Company's First Squad, Third Platoon, had lost two of its men to nonfatal wounds. Others in that squad and in Company K would not be as lucky as Willie Shimabukuro and Al Terney.

Enemy fire—mortars, machine guns, and small arms—pinned them down all that day. With night

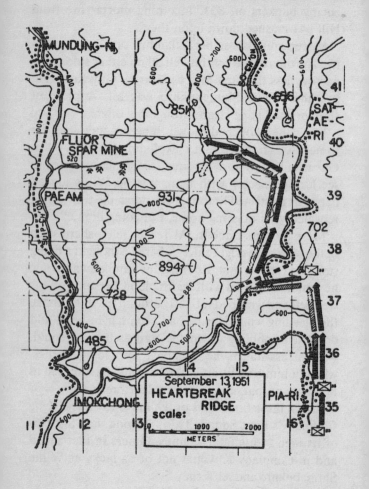

Map 3
Unit movements, September 13, 1951

coming on, they were forced to form a perimeter defense and dig in where they were. But digging in was not easy because the ground was so rocky.

Early that morning B Company had intercepted an enemy radio message in Korean. The interpreted message said that very night the North Koreans would launch a three-battalion attack. One battalion coming down from Hill 894, one battalion from Hill 931, and a third attacking from the north down the main supply route (MSR) would "clean out the valley."[13]

"Clean out the valley" meant ridding it of the Third and Second Battalion, (3/23 and 2/23), which had penetrated it that day. Second Battalion had moved out from its assembly area that morning at 0700 hours. Its progress was delayed due to the Third Battalion action, but in the early afternoon G "George" Company followed by F "Fox" Company crossed the LD. Like Third Battalion, Second Battalion (2/23) also came under automatic weapons fire from enemy bunkers located on the east slopes of Hill 931 and had to stop. G and F Companies tied in with Third Battalion's companies for the night.

And so if the earlier translated message proved accurate and an attack by experienced night fighters did come, the Twenty-third's pinned-down infantry could all be easily wiped out.

They waited. In the darkness the weary and dispirited men were encouraged by Colonel Adams's tall figure moving among them. But the enemy attack did not materialize, and except for a fire fight with 15 to 20 probing enemy in G Company's area and the ambush around midnight of a supply party on its way to Second Battalion, that night remained relatively quiet.

Customarily Brigadier General de Shazo talked every night around ten P.M. to the X Corps commander, General Byers, about that day's operations. Of the first day's assault, he reported: "Everything is all right. We didn't get up on top of the ridge. They are fighting a nonorganized resistance." He then outlined Second Division's plans for the next day, which included putting the Ninth Regiment into action. Byers's response was positive: "That is wonderful, Tom."[14]

When daylight broke on September 14, the Twenty-third began moving again along the rocky spur. As they came closer to the ridge's crest between the middle hill (931) and the north hill (851), the gray fog began to lift a little. Suddenly everywhere, in front, behind, and beside every soldier, mortar rounds—all calibers—were bursting and throwing up dirt, rock, and hot shrapnel.

Heavy enemy mortar and artillery concentrations on the attacking units of Twenty-third Regiment continued throughout the morning of September 14, inflicting heavy casualties. In midafternoon L Company with I Company following attacked up the finger leading to the ridge connecting Hills 931 and 851.

With his characteristic flair, the Third Battalion commander, Major Craven, sent this message to the Twenty-third Regiment commander, Colonel Adams:

Have uncoiled and struck behind rolling artillery barrage. Enemy crust is broken. Fast moving

situation. Line extended. Need flank and rear
security. Trying to cut ridge tonight.[15]

Adams was nonplussed. He understood all his
commanders well. Not long after he had taken command of the Twenty-third Infantry Regiment in early
July, a newly assigned major—tall, over six feet, but
not nearly as tall or slender as Adams himself—
reported to him. "Sir, I am Virgil E. 'Gene' Craven,
and I am a-craving for a fight."

"God damn," thought Adams, "I ought to send this
brash young man right back where he came from."

He also thought the major appeared too mild to be a
combat soldier. Craven was in fact a 1941 Reserve
Officers Training Corps (ROTC) graduate of Kansas
State College, and during World War II he had distin-
guished himself in action as a company commander
in the Thirty-fourth Infantry Division during the
African and Italian Campaigns.

Colonel Adams's initial reservations about his new
battalion commander soon changed. On one occasion
the regimental commander reluctantly had to convey
a message from the division commander to Major
Craven. The order was that Craven's battalion, which
had just taken some ground, was to pull back. Craven's response, "I'll be a son of a bitch if I will,
Colonel." Right then and there Adams decided that
Gene Craven was going to make a fine battalion
commander; and in the colonel's estimation he did
indeed show himself to be a splendid commander.[16]

But in the present instance, Major Craven's message proved overly optimistic. Third battalion did not

cut the ridge that day. The enemy's "crust" was far from broken.

By 1715 hours the advance had carried Third Battalion only a few hundred yards when the defending North Koreans zeroed in with a heavy barrage of 82-mm mortar fire, saturating the area with hot, deadly steel. Still short of its objective, the beleaguered battalion halted at 2000 hours to dig in for the night.

A little earlier it had been erroneously reported that Third Battalion had cut the ridgeline between Hills 931 and 851. In response to this good news, Second Battalion was ordered forward to reinforce its sister battalion. Although it was soon learned that the report was false, Second Battalion was instructed to continue its move forward. In the wee hours of the morning E Company reached positions to tie in with Third Battalion, and by 0445 hours all of Second Battalion's companies reached positions to tie in for what little time of darkness remained.

After two days of fighting, Twenty-third Infantry Regiment with its attached French Battalion sustained 75 battle casualties. But the two hills, 931 and 851, had not been taken. Not only that, the connecting ridgeline between these two hills had not yet been reached.

There was no certainty that in exchange for these casualties any worthwhile injury had been inflicted upon the enemy. Twelve prisoners-of-war (POWs) had been taken, but anything else was a guess: At most, perhaps, 20 North Koreans had been killed and a like number wounded.

The acting commanding general, Second Division, belatedly became worried about Twenty-third's men exposed out on the ridge all night. He exhorted Colonel Walker, Divarty commanding officer, "This is the most important night for Second Divarty since they have been in Korea. You have got to protect that area and don't let anything hit them. You people must keep them protected within 600 yards."

He then reported to General Byers, "It was bad news all day but toward dark it started getting better."

The X Corps commander tried to encourage him: "That is how it goes, but I think you have it cracked now."

And de Shazo promised, "Tomorrow we will clear it up."[17]

When the morning of September 15 came, Item Company took the lead in Craven's Third Battalion with Love and King Companies following. Foot by foot the men crawled up the steep, rocky slopes. Small arms and automatic weapons fire came at them from all directions. The incessant firing was from concealed enemy bunkers. At 1230 Item Company was just 200 feet short of the ridgeline. There it was halted by a withering hail of bullets.

Meanwhile Second Battalion's Easy Company swung south of Item's position in an attempt to remove the pressure being exerted from the west upon that pinned-down company. At 1600 hours Easy was joined by Fox moving to its left to give support by fire.

Now both Second Battalion companies came under heavy mortar fire from the enemy. But Easy Company was stalled for about two hours. When able to resume its advance, it eventually reached the ridgeline and moved south toward the nose of the north knob of Hill 931.

The North Koreans were prepared for this, however. Easy found itself surrounded with fire coming in from four sides. Complete annihilation was a near reality before they were able to extricate themselves from this trap.

The two battalions (2/23 and 3/23) dug in for their third uneasy night on the unyielding ridgeline. Despite all, Brigadier General de Shazo's report to General Byers that night was still optimistic.

De Shazo: "Adams is right down into the bunkers. They will continue over there tomorrow."

Byers: "Do you think that one will collapse completely tomorrow?"

De Shazo: "I'm sure, sir."[18]

While Adams's Twenty-third Regiment was making repeatedly unsuccessful assaults against Hills 931 and 851, Col. John Lynch's Ninth Infantry Regiment was positioned southeastward of the main hill mass (851, 931, and 894) near Pia-ri. The Ninth's mission was to move onto Hill 728, located about 1,800 meters southwest of Hill 894. Brigadier General de Shazo's initial plan was for the Ninth to move onto Hill 728 *after* the Twenty-third had secured its assigned objective. This would conclude the Second Division's hold of the whole rocky range.

Although the Ninth had been contributing to the action of the Twenty-third on the ridgeline with a base of fire employing recoilless rifles, mortars, and .50-caliber machine guns, the acting division commander in his report to the X Corps commander on the night of September 13 told him: "I think it is time to put the Ninth in action now."

Immediately after de Shazo got off the telephone to General Byers, he got in touch with Colonel Lynch, commanding the Ninth Regiment, and ordered, "I want you to move your battalion at first daylight and coordinate with Adams." He told Lynch, "Get your people around there, coordinate and move right up there."[19]

Complying with these orders, Lynch moved his Second Battalion less F Company (2/9-F) against Hill 728. They had fire support from the 4.2-inch mortars and the attached tanks from B Company, Seventy-second Tank Battalion. Moving forward under moderate long-range fire from the enemy on Hill 894, the battalion by 1200 hours had reached a point on the southeast slope of 894 about 1,300 meters southwest of Santae-dong.

A little less than two hours later they were on top of the ridgeline running south from Hill 894. The Ninth was then ordered to attack that hill from the south, mutually supporting the Twenty-third Regiment in its effort to the north. Although constantly under hostile small arms fire, this northeast advance carried them to a point about 650 meters south-southwest of Hill 894's crest. There, G and E Companies formed a perimeter defense for the night.

Success crowned the Ninth Infantry's efforts on September 15. Jumping off at 0700, the Second Battalion (2/9) took Hill 894 after eight hours of hard fighting, despite heavy enemy automatic weapons fire cutting through their entire force. In these efforts Second Battalion (2/9) took many casualties. Sgt. Dale E. Hall from Michigan, a medical company aid man attached to Company E, Ninth Regiment, saw several wounded men unattended, lying in an area swept over by constant enemy small arms fire. Courageously he crawled out to them and, going from one to the other, began treating their injuries. Sergeant Hall himself was hit but refused to be evacuated, not until all his comrades had been cared for and moved to safer ground.[20]

George Company of the Second Battalion (2/23) led off the attack very early on September 16. Moving out at 0530, its progress was slow, for again the company met intense enemy small arms and automatic weapons fire. That morning the advancing troops encountered an additional obstacle. A carefully laid enemy minefield blocked George Company's avenue of approach. Not only did the men face the possibility of exploding mines under their feet, but the North Koreans were covering the field with automatic weapons firing out of the many bunkers honeycombing the area. There was nothing to do but skirt the field. And so George Company moved to a new approach route. But now it was about dark, and the men were ordered to halt and tie in for the night.

Meanwhile Item Company had moved out at 0630.

Moving along the lateral-extending finger leading to the ridgeline, they were met with a rattle of machine guns and crack of AK rifles coming from out of the North Korean bunkers. They stopped and called in friendly artillery.

The artillery forward observers took over to radio back instructions, bringing in well-precisioned and adjusted fire that, one by one, systematically knocked out the bunkers. The enemy bunkers erupted in flame and debris under impact of high-explosive 155-mm shells. Finally, at 1600 hours, the enemy was silenced.

By 1900 hours Item Company was organizing to renew its assault. Enemy mortar shells began erupting all around them, and several men were hit. Swarming down off Hill 851, about 25 North Koreans were firing their burp guns full blast. This counterattack lasted only 15 minutes before it was successfully repulsed; nonetheless Item suffered many casualties.

The surrounding rugged peaks closed out the sun, and darkness came on early along this part of Korea's 38th parallel. Another day ended with ridgeline and hills still in enemy hands. Colonel Adams gave Brigadier General de Shazo a detailed update of the situation, reporting that his companies were reducing the enemy bunkers. De Shazo informed Adams that General Van Fleet, the Eighth Army commander, had visited the Second Division command post that day and had stated that "if we were smart we would just keep getting these bunkers without taking casualties doing it." Obviously the Eighth Army commander still thought that the enemy bunkers could be knocked out by artillery fire.

Adams reported that most of his casualties were from mortar fire. De Shazo then inquired about any observation of enemy activity and expressed his concern, declaring, "I am afraid if we don't get it tomorrow we may have to fight more reinforcements."[21]

This fear proved all too correct, for that very day General Hong Nim, the N.K. *Sixth Division* commander, had replaced his N.K. *First Regiment,* which had been battered so severely by U.S. attacks, with a whole fresh regiment—the N.K. *Thirteenth.*

Brigadier General de Shazo, in turn, reported to his superior, "Some progress, not a complete success."

It was becoming clear to all that ultimate capture of this ridgeline and these hills would be no easy task. There was no lack of fire support. But would battalion-size frontal attacks be able to neutralize the firmly entrenched enemy?

War correspondents had gotten word of the bitter fighting now taking place at this point on the U.N. line. Capt. Louis-Christian Michelet, the French liaison officer to the Twenty-third Regiment, was standing beside its commander, the tall colonel who so many times and in so many ways had shown his personal concern for his men. Speaking now to one reporter, Adams, with deep feeling, was heard to say, "To send battalion after battalion up this ridge only to have them slaughtered, with no reinforcements to back them up, is such a heartbreak for me."[22]

That word, *heartbreak,* caught the correspondent's ear, and so he used it in his story about the terrible fighting on these desolate hills in far-off Korea, where scores of men were being killed every day. Other journalists picked up the descriptive word. Soon Heartbreak Ridge found its way into official reports and was on the lips of the men who through their human sacrifice ensured that for so many, these hills and the bitter struggle taking place on them were indeed a heartbreak.

4

The Assault Continues

> You can say that you have experienced something equal to Verdun.
>
> *General Ralph Monclar,*
> *Commander, French Forces in Korea[1]*

To exploit the gains made the day before by the Second Battalion, Ninth Infantry (2/9), Colonel Adams had dispatched C Company of the Twenty-third's First Battalion (1/23) to pass through Ninth's G Company, which was entrenched on Hill 894.

C Company was to continue the attack to the north up the ridge to Hill 931. Upon clearing G Company's positions, C Company met heavy enemy small arms fire coming from bunkers on the 931 Hill mass. Friendly artillery fire was called in to knock out the bunkers, and C Company prepared night positions.

As C Company began digging in, Company A of the First Battalion (1/23) was designated as C Company's backup. To accomplish this, Company A was moved into position southeast of C.

Throughout the long night the tired Twenty-third infantrymen got no rest. A heavy mortar barrage exploded on the Third Battalion around 2300 hours, and L Company was the object of a North Korean two-platoon probing attack. Midnight came. As September 16 passed into the 17th, the enemy attack increased in size. L Company's losses were heavy. Despite that, they held their defenses and the North Koreans were repulsed. Each of the Twenty-third's three battalions on line received enemy probing attacks to feel out their strength and pinpoint their positions. The strongest attacks were made against C Company; and at 0300 hours on September 17 these probing attacks developed into a full-scale assault by a battalion-size force of North Koreans.

C Company's ammunition began to run low. Carrying parties bringing up a resupply were scattered by enemy mortar fire. Finally some of the defenders in the most outlying positions ran out of ammunition and were overrun. A few tried fighting off their attackers with bare fists, allowing their buddies to pull back to better positions, where they could get ammunition from A Company.

When dawn broke A Company moved up to reinforce C and to share with them some of their ammunition. It was altogether fitting that A was the one to come to C's aid, for the C Company commander, First Lieutenant Juneau, had been a platoon leader in A just before being designated to take over leadership of the sister company.

Linus Mark Juneau, a "full-blooded Cajun," had grown up in Avoyelles Parish, Louisiana. In September 1940, at the age of 18, he enlisted in the U.S. Army. In December 1942 he was commissioned a second lieutenant after going through Officers Candidate School (O.C.S.) at Fort Benning, Georgia. He was then assigned to Second Infantry Division and saw combat in the European theater as a platoon leader in a rifle company.

Juneau left the army at the end of World War II, but with the outbreak of the Korean War in 1950, he again volunteered. He specifically requested assignment to his old division, the Second, and specifically to the Twenty-third Regiment because he knew its then commanding officer, Colonel Chiles, who had been Second Division general staff for operations (G-3).

Mortar, small arms, and automatic weapons fire began pouring in upon both A and C Companies at 1130 hours. Thirty minutes later the North Koreans launched a two-company attack against them. The U.S. forces stubbornly held their ground and drove the attackers back, in the process inflicting many casualties upon the enemy.

If Lieutenant Juneau had anything more to learn about fighting and leadership—which he probably didn't, for he had already exhibited those martial qualities of his French ancestry and might have fit in quite well as a member of the French Battalion—he would have learned it in A Company. A Company—Able—of the Twenty-third Regiment was blessed with the best leadership any company could hope to have.

It is unlikely that the trio, the company's commanding officer (CO) and two of its noncommissioned officers, with their diverse backgrounds would have gotten together under any circumstances other than war. But war sometimes brings together strange bedfellows, and here in these barren hills of Korea a friendship and camaraderie formed between Jim Dick, Chuck Rothenberg, and Nick Nicholas that would last their lifetimes.

James Dick, of an athletic build and a little less than average height, was a 33-year-old captain when he took command of A Company, Twenty-third Regiment, on June 10, 1951. He had known since the age of 14 that he was career military. That was when as a high school freshman he entered Greenbriar Military School at Lewisburg, West Virginia, after having spent his early years in Elizabeth, New Jersey, with his father (Jim's mother had died when he was in fifth grade).

After completing high school, Dick went through senior ROTC at Greenbriar and upon graduation was commissioned a second lieutenant at the age of 21. Then January 1940 found him at Fort Benning, Georgia, where he transferred to Airborne and took parachute training. During World War II he served in the Pacific theater as a company officer in 503d Parachute Regiment. On duty with the Military District of New York and New Jersey at the outbreak of the Korean War, Dick volunteered for an infantry division because he thought he would see more combat action in infantry than with a parachute outfit.

He would not be disappointed. In Twenty-third Regiment, Second Division, Jim Dick was to see as much fierce fighting as anyone anywhere in Korea.

Charles "Chuck" Rothenberg, Jewish, tall, dark-haired and blue-eyed, with prominent nose, had a big-city background—Chicago. He was at 23 a college graduate—and a draftee who "didn't particularly care for the army and didn't really know what he was doing here in Korea."[2]

When Captain Dick took command, Chuck Rothenberg was A Company's orderly room clerk. Dick saw in him managerial potential, and wanting to be free of day-to-day administrative details so that he could command his company out on the line with his troops, Dick jumped the greenhorn private all the way up to first sergeant. Chuck ran the orderly room well and so proved his leadership abilities that he later functioned fully as first sergeant on the line.

Many saw in Gaither "Nick" Nicholas a similarity to Sergeant York of World War I fame. The tall and lanky 23-year-old master sergeant from Crossville in the mountains of East Tennessee had grown up with a squirrel rifle in his hands. An expert rifle shot, he was now platoon leader of First Platoon—the only platoon leader in A Company that was not a commissioned officer. Captain Dick had earlier relieved the lieutenant platoon leader when that officer refused to obey an order and in his place he put Sgt. Nicholas. (Dick noted that the former platoon leader's disobedience was the single exception to an outstanding performance by all officers and enlisted men he knew throughout his time in Korea.)

Each of the three—Nick Nicholas, Chuck Rothenberg, and Jim Dick, their commanding officer— would suffer a like fate. Each would earn a Purple Heart on Heartbreak Ridge, but the wounds of one of them would be serious indeed.

Following their bloody encounter with the North Koreans on September 16, I Company's ranks were badly depleted and in need of replacements. One of the new men coming into the unit, Jack Fisher, must have set a record for time from stateside to combat. He had been activated into the United States Army with the call-up of the Thirty-first Alabama National Guard Division in January 1951. After completing his training with the division at Fort Jackson, S.C., and enjoying a 30-day leave in his hometown of Prattesville, Alabama, he was on his way to Seattle, Washington, on individual orders to Korea. Just seven days before his arrival on Heartbreak Ridge, Jack Fisher had been in Seattle. Going from there by train to Vancouver, British Columbia, he flew on Canadian Pacific Airlines to Tokyo and then rode by train to Sasebo, ferry to Pusan, train to Taegu, and truck to Heartbreak Ridge.

Climbing up the mountainside, guided by a returning I Company man who had been wounded earlier,

Fisher encountered machine-gun fire, not to mention the single mortar round that interrupted his lunch of C-rations. When he finally arrived in the company area, he saw dead bodies from the fire fight of the night before still awaiting evacuation. The new replacement would take part in the very next combat action by I Company.

At 1345 hours on September 17 Item of 3/23—I Company—launched an attack along the east ridge leading to the main hill mass. Immediately enemy machine-gun fire from the north ripped into them. Item's machine gunners used their own weapons to neutralize one North Korean bunker. Then 57-mm recoilless rifle gunners destroyed other enemy bunkers.

The 57-mm rifle firing a high-explosive cartridge has a maximum range of about 1,900 yards with a bursting area of 340 yards. However, to be effective against one of the hardened North Korean bunkers, its gunner had to be so accurate as to send his projectile through a two-foot by two-foot opening that the enemy gunner used for firing his weapon. Impact against the bunker's timber-reinforced, sandbagged walls produced no results.

Moving forward again, Item next faced a thick blanket of hand grenades thrown upon it. This time the men used a 75-mm recoilless rifle to reduce the impeding bunker. The maximum effective range of the 75-mm is about 200 yards greater than that of the 57-mm and its effective bursting area is nearly twice as large as the 57's. Even with this better performance, the 75's gunner likewise had to accurately fire a projectile right through the small opening for the bunker's own weapon.

Third Battalion had two companies on the east ridge by 2105 hours before it established night positions.

Earlier, just as Second Battalion was preparing at 1000 hours that morning to attack Hill 931 from the west, it was hit by a 30-round enemy mortar barrage. E Company jumped off on schedule, though, and at 1300 F Company moved over to the right of E while G remained in position to support both of the other two companies with fire.

As Easy was approaching the north knob of the 931 Hill mass, more mortar and small arms fire were directed against it. In the face of such a barrier of fire, E could advance no farther and was ordered to pull back.

It was now 1730 hours. The men were told to dig in. So right away Carl Kleinpeter started working with his fellow ammo bearer to prepare themselves a two-man foxhole.

Just a few days before, Carl had been forced to split up from his first cousin, Olen, by whose side he had been every day since coming to Korea—carrying ammunition, eating, sleeping, going for water; actually side by side every day since joining the army together.

Their platoon leader, Lieutenant Pillsbury, had called them aside.

"Kleinpeter. That's not a common name. You must be kin."

"No, no, we ain't," they lied, because they wanted to stay together.

"Where are you from?"

They looked at each other with sly grins on their faces and then answered truthfully, "East Baton Rouge, Louisiana, sir."

"Both from the same place. How much kin are you?"

When they admitted they were first cousins, Pillsbury continued, "From now on, you two can no longer be together. It might be that one of you would see the other get killed, and that wouldn't be right."[3]

At the moment Carl was digging furiously with his entrenching tool that had a shovel on one end and a pick on the other. His new partner was prying at the rocks trying to loosen them and pull them out to place around the outside rim of their foxhole for added protection. They had dug about 12 or 14 inches deep when they hit an especially big rock. Uncovering more dirt, all they found were bigger rocks.

Just then, a deafening roar and a thundering crunch. Then more. Mortars were falling around them making the very earth tremble under their feet. Already the enemy had zeroed in on their night position. There was burp-gun fire, too, but the bullets were just strays because as yet the North Koreans were not close in. If close enough, a burp gun's bullets could cut a man in half.

Carl felt a ripping pain and heard a pop as a burp gun's bullet exploded in his gut. It had entered through the left lower part of his abdomen. Immediately he lifted his fatigue jacket to have a look. Blood was oozing out of the hole, and although he saw no intestines, he knew instinctively somehow—maybe it was the popping sound like a bursting balloon—that his intestines had been punctured.

But there was something that captured Carl's attention more so than his injury and pain. Less than six feet away, simultaneously with his own wounding, a mortar round had hit one of his comrades in the shoulder. The man's right arm was completely severed, blown right away. Blood spurted everywhere and everyone was screaming, "Medic, medic."

Carl heard someone shout, "Get back! Go back!"

Go back where? All around him there was nothing but other shallow foxholes like the one he had been working on.

After one brief, curious look, he had pulled his fatigue jacket back down and clasped both hands over the gaping wound. Then he walked. He walked with the man with no arm, down over a little rise.

The medics gave them shots of morphine and placed them on litters to be carried to the battalion aid station. The ride was bumpy as the litter bearers kept stumbling over rocks and tree stubbles—the result of repeated bombardments.

Although they had been "split up," Olen was at that very same time carrying ammunition to another heavy machine-gun position, also in Easy Company. He had just set his boxes of ammunition down and turned to go for more when a mortar round impacted near him. Olen felt instant pain as several mortar fragments splattered over his back. He felt blood running down his back. A medic tried to put him on a litter, but Olen insisted on walking down the ridgeline to the aid station.

Ironically Olen and Carl were leaving Heartbreak Ridge at exactly the same time. They would be in the battalion aid station together without either one knowing the other was there. Each learned of the other's injuries only when they later corresponded, Olen from a hospital in Pusan and Carl from Japan.

Olen would return to Heartbreak Ridge just as the bloody operation ended; Carl would never see Heartbreak again.

Battle casualties (the killed and wounded) that day in Twenty-third Regiment were as follows: First Battalion, 29; Second Battalion, 13; Third Battalion, 23; and the French Battalion, 3.

At 1000 hours on September 18 Lieutenant Juneau jumped off with his Company C determined to retake the knob of Hill 931 from which they had been driven the day before. They fought hard for three hours against small arms and mortar fire, and in the end were successful. The overrun machine-gun positions where men had died fighting with bare fists were recaptured. They counted 53 enemy killed in action (KIA).

Now a new tactic to dislodge the North Koreans was decided upon—a night assault. While still light, on September 18, Third Battalion (3/23) was resupplied and made other preparations. Second Battalion (2/23) adjusted its positions to better support the

Third, and in First Battalion (1/23) Capt. Jim Dick of
A Company and Capt. Willie Jordan of B Company
moved their two companies to more advanced positions from which to attack.

Major Craven chose Love Company to lead the
Third Battalion night action (see Map 4). Love's
company commander was a bright, personable, handsome young officer, 1st Lt. Peter H. Monfore, a 1950
graduate of West Point. Earlier in the year when Pete
Monfore had been in the regiment's S-3 section he
earned a reputation among his fellow lieutenants as
always being considerate and helpful. Most of the
other lieutenants were reservists, and for them the
military was a second profession. They welcomed
guidance from a West Pointer, a "real" military
professional. And Lieutenant Monfore did not disap-
point them. All his fellow officers were impressed by
his sincere interest in all things having to do with
infantry.

But what the aggressive and ambitious lieutenant
wanted most was to lead a company on the line. A day
or so before the 18th, Pete Monfore had told Lt. Dick
Kotite, First Battalion Headquarters Company CO,
that now that he was a company commander, he was
"very happy."[4]

Now, on the evening of September 18, the prime
focus was on Love Company and its young commander. Hopes ran high that the upcoming night assault
would at long last spell the end to this whole heart-
rending affair.

At 2030 hours Love passed through Item

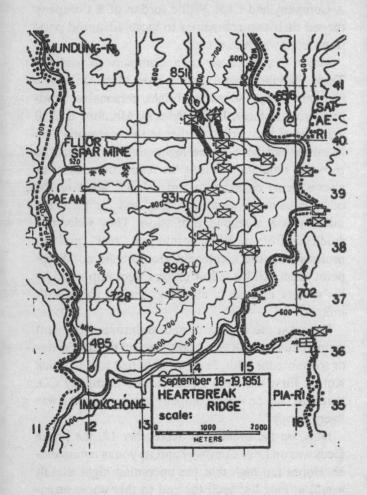

Map 4
Unit movements, September 18–19, 1951

Company's positions and advanced to the first knob on the way to Heartbreak. Flashes of yellow-red light appeared all around like so many giant fireflies as machine guns broke the silence with their deadly staccato rattle. As their .30-caliber bullets ripped through Love Company's ranks, Monfore and his men did not slow their movement forward. They knew that they were now right in among the enemy's bunkers, and the bunkers would have to be taken out before Love could go on to its prized objective.

Flame throwers proved ideal for the job. Held at waist level much like a machine gun, the portable flame thrower was operated by one man who carried on his back a four-gallon, 25–29-pound tank of thick liquid fluid. Pressurized gas propelled this fluid outward in a burning molten jet to a distance of 40 yards. The flame's intense heat ignited and charred anything inflammable it hit. It also seared human flesh.

Operating this weapon, U.S. fighting men in World War II had effectively routed out fanatical Japanese from their Pacific Island caves. Now North Koreans, otherwise secure in their cavelike bunkers, would experience its deadly effects. For the weapon to be effective, however, there was one critical ingredient—the flame thrower operator had to get in close enough.

L Company approached the second knob at 2120 hours, still using their flame throwers to flush out the enemy defenders. Ten minutes later the division forward command post got a report that the determined company was going up the third and last knob and drawing quite a bit of enemy small arms fire. At 2145 hours friendly artillery fire that had been rolling ahead of the leading columns shifted to fire on the reverse slope of Hill 851.

Once on the ridge Love turned north, headed for that night's final objective. Soon Item topped the ridge, prepared to follow Love onto Hill 851. King moved right behind Item, followed by Fox and George. All was going well. Unbelievably, the battalion had suffered no casualties thus far.

In the final two hours Pete Monfore and his men fought bitterly in an exchange of small arms fire with the North Koreans. Yellow streaks from tracer bullets swept back and forth in deathly brilliance. Machine guns rattled angrily. But at last the prize was won: They were atop Hill 851, and the enemy was fleeing, disappearing in the darkness down the hill's other side.

Lieutenant Monfore gave the order to form a perimeter defense. Immediately the men paired off and began digging furiously. They soon had foxholes ready. Then machine-gun and mortar crews set up emplacements for their weapons. Although exhausted, everyone was satisfied that they had accomplished their goal. And best of all the job had been done with only three casualties in Third Battalion. In contrast, the estimate for enemy killed in action was over 50, and there were also 21 North Korean prisoners of war.

It was now past midnight. Only sporadically did a single mortar or artillery round break the calm of those early morning hours to land near Love's well-prepared perimeter. Suddenly, out of the darkness, the enemy struck. First a company of screaming enemy soldiers came up the hill, firing their weapons full blast. (Many of the weapons were Soviet-made .47s.) Laying down a field of accurate fire, Monfore's men turned them back. But then came a full battalion, later identified as being from the N.K. *Fifteenth Regiment, Sixth Division.* As L Company's fire cut down wave after wave of attacking enemy, Hong Nim recklessly threw in fresh replacements. The enemy seemed to be drawing from a bottomless pit of North Korean reserves. And always ready to back them up were the Chinese "volunteers," hundreds of thousands strong.

The enemy got in between L and I Companies. After that, it was all a bloody slaughter.

A deep saddle or draw separated King from Love, but the two companies were in contact through an EE-8 telephone hookup. The EE-8 served as an efficient means of communication as long as the connecting communications wire remained intact. A problem arose when mortar and artillery fire, as it frequently did, cut the wire.

At this time the hookup between L and K functioned well. K's only two officers on line, the company commander, 1st Lt. Lloyd Payne, and 1st Lt. Bill Williams, the platoon leader of the Third Platoon, had been keeping tabs on L's progress. About 0400 hours "all hell broke loose," in the words of Bill Williams. Lieutenant Monfore came on the phone excitedly. "We are being hit with everything I've ever seen."

"What's your situation?" asked Lieutenant Payne.

"We are dug in well," replied Monfore, "but 60-mm mortars are falling right on our foxholes."

Very shortly he called back. "I think we are about to be overrun. Send us some help."

Before King could respond, Love's top sergeant, 1st Sgt. Sun, a Hawaiian, was on the phone. "Lieutenant Monfore has been hit. All our other officers are dead. We are desperate for help."

Sergeant Sun sounded as if he was in shock.

Lieutenant Williams immediately offered to go. Using the communications wire as a guide, with an enlisted man (EM) volunteer, he worked his way across the deep saddle up to L Company's positions on Hill 851.

What Bill Williams found was a desperate state indeed. Pete Monfore was dead. The body was laid out, supine, the shirt open to reveal a single round hole in the middle of his chest, the entrance wound where a sniper's bullet had found its mark. The bullet had missed the little Bible which the lieutenant always carried in a bulletproof metal case in his shirt's left pocket. There was very little blood, and Pete had died instantly. Many other bodies lay all around, both North Korean and U.S.

First Sergeant Sun talked in short, broken sentences. He was suffering from concussion caused by a mortar round falling close to him. Assuming command of Company L, Bill Williams ordered that Sun be taken back to the battalion aid station.

There were only 55 effectives left in the whole company; perhaps, only 12 or 14 men were completely whole. Ironically they still held the 21 North Korean prisoners.

Lieutenant Williams's main thought was to get everyone safely off the exposed hill; but when he got on the telephone, he learned that battalion was insisting they stay in place. Just then, "fortunately" (his word) the telephone wire became severed, leaving him to act on his own.[5]

I Company placed grazing machine-gun fire on those enemy positions located on the highest ground of Hill 851, allowing the remnants of L Company to pull back. Poles cut from saplings with a shelter half stretched between them served as an improvised litter to carry Monfore's body.

The battered party was about 25 yards from K Company when enemy 120-mm mortar rounds began falling upon them. Two of the men carrying their dead commanding officer were hit with shrapnel. An exploding round blew body and litter down a rocky cliff. Mortars continued coming in as the men crawled the rest of the way to where K Company was located. The mortar barrage threw up broken rock and pebbles that themselves became destructive missiles, and one of these hit Bill Williams on his right knee, chipping a bone. Daylight had broken through when the party got back to K Company's positions.

One might think that in this situation death and the ever presence of dead bodies would have been so commonplace that one more corpse would hold no special meaning. However, for the men of Third Battalion it did not seem right that a company commander's body, especially when that body was completely intact, should be left to lie out there and decay in no-man's-land.

And so Pfc. Guy Robinson and his good friend Pfc. Al Seghetti, along with two of the men from L Company who had returned with Lt. Williams, volunteered to go out with Sgt. Cliff Karlson, assistant squad leader of their squad, to retrieve Lt. Monfore's body. The five men started crawling out well aware that they were placing themselves in added danger. With mortar rounds constantly falling and sniper bullets striking the ground all around them, they crawled out about 20 yards when over the deafening sounds they heard Sgt. Karlson yelling to them, "Guy, Al, stop! Go back." They crawled back disappointed, but with some satisfaction that at least they had tried.

Third Battalion (3/23) withdrew some 800 meters south of the objective. E and F of Second Battalion (2/23) passed through and counterattacked the enemy to take pressure off Third Battalion. The advance was stopped by a barrage of 120-mm mortar and intense automatic weapons fire from bunkers on the slopes of Hill 851, which had been rapidly reoccupied by the North Koreans.

Still more mortars fell on K Company that day. The Third Platoon sergeant, M. Sgt. George Anderson, was hit by shrapnel in the face, both arms, and back. The back wound was the most serious, for a piece of steel had entered one lung, collapsing it. On impact he was knocked to the ground and could hardly take a breath. No complainer, he nevertheless found that hollering somehow helped him to breathe more easily.

He was taken first to the battalion aid station where his chest was taped and then to a mobile army surgical hospital (MASH) unit to be operated upon. After a 30-day stay in Osaka, Japan, he was back in the United States. By the end of the year he was out of the army.

Sgt. Cliff Karlson took over as Third Platoon's acting platoon sergeant. By midafternoon, Lt. Williams's right leg was swollen so badly that he, too, had to be evacuated for medical treatment.

At the same time that L Company, Third Battalion (3/23), was receiving its baptism by fire on Hill 851, First Battalion's (1/23) A Company prepared to attack Hill 931 from the south, moving out at 0310 hours. In the early morning hours the North Koreans made A the object of a probing attack, but that company drove the enemy off after a brief fire fight.

Captain Dick led his men through C Company's positions and A had advanced only 50 yards when they became engaged in another small arms fire fight. Although in constant contact with the enemy, the company continued to move forward and by 0634 hours two platoons of A were across a draw leading to Hill 931. Two hours later Dick's company was about 300 yards to the left of the high point of 931 and approximately two-thirds of the way from the top when mortar rounds (120-mm) began hitting them. Captain Dick called for 155-mm artillery fire on Hill 931.

Peering through that early morning's gray fog, using their binoculars to scan the terrain in front of them, forward observers spotted an enemy bunker. Out of this bunker flashed yellow-red bursts of light from three or four machine guns. The observers also thought they saw a 51-mm mountain gun.

A Company gunners brought up a .57-mm recoilless rifle, and with a loud whoosh and an acrid backfire the rifle sent its 2.25-pound projectile against the enemy bunker, then another and another—eight in one minute. The bunker remained intact. Next First Battalion sent over 81-mm mortar rounds to fall on the enemy bunker. Still it was not destroyed. Tragically, the artillery fire intended for the enemy fell short and destructive shells began landing in A Company's area, so that several A Company men were killed or wounded by this "friendly fire."

M. Sgt. Gaither Nicholas's First Platoon had several killed and wounded in this fighting on September 19, but to Sgt. Nicholas it seemed that he and his fellow Tennesseans were survivors. Making it through the deadly fire unharmed were, besides himself, Tennesseans Sanders, Koons, and Cullum Dossett, son-in-law of that famous country-western singer Roy Acuff.

A Company was effectively stalled, unable to advance any farther that day. Meanwhile B and C Companies had moved up behind A. In the afternoon an enemy force 200 strong struck both Able and Baker (A and B Companies). Defensive mortar fires successfully turned them back, though.

Jim Dick kept a diary while in Korea. Understandably, he could make only abbreviated entries while leading Company A in daily combat. On this day he recorded the following:

19 Sept.—Attack Hill 931 (Heartbreak Ridge).
50 WIA, 4 KIA. Lt. Griffin KIA instantly by a
mortar. Lt. Steel WIA.

These entries, though brief, would serve to recall to
Dick's mind dramatic events that, because there were
so many of them occurring one on top of the other,
might otherwise have been pushed back into his
subconscious. The Lieutenant Steel who was wounded this day had reported to duty just three days before,
on September 16.

Right in the middle of the fire fight, as mortars were
falling all around, Captain Dick took a telephone call
from Colonel Adams. Characteristically, the tall colonel had some news that he wanted to relay personally.

"Jim, this is Adams."

"Yes, sir."

"I want you to get in touch with Lieutenant Griffin
and tell him his wife has just had a baby boy."[6]

Jim Dick immediately tried to contact the lieutenant, who was from Bradford, Pennsylvania. He
reached, instead, the platoon's radio operator who
told him, "Lieutenant Griffin has just been killed."

Dick was stunned by the details related to him. The
Lieutenant's head had been blown off by a mortar
round. As told by the men who saw it, the body
without a head stood perfectly erect for several seconds after that.

There were other events that needed no written
record to be recalled, so indelibly were they imprinted
upon the mind. Jim Dick himself saw something (also
witnessed by Chuck Rothenberg) that was so amazing

it defied human imagination.[7] An enlisted man, an Hispanic, was running up a hill when a 60-mm mortar round exploded, blowing off both the man's feet at his ankles. The man just continued running on the stumps of his legs for 15 more yards before collapsing.

First Battalion had at least one other diarist on Heartbreak. Pvt. Raymond Myers from Brimfield, Illinois, a 19-year-old high school dropout (he had gone through eighth grade and part of the ninth) sensed the historical significance of the situation he was in and what he was doing. He kept a little notebook in which he jotted down events important to him. On this same day he wrote:

9/19 They threw artillery on us all day. I just about got it. I stayed in the bunker all day. I was scared to death. I had a piece hit my windshield.

A piece of steel striking his jeep upset Raymond about as much as getting hit himself. The cocky young man took great pride in the jeep he drove about for Maj. George Williams, the First Battalion commander.

Twenty-third Regiment's battle casualties (the killed and wounded) for the 24-hour period were as follows: First Battalion, 64; Second Battalion, 13; Third Battalion, 48; and the French Battalion, 5. The regiment had taken 44 POWs from units of the N. K. *Sixth Division.*

5

. . . And Continues

Heartbreak Ridge—without question the most savage single action of the Korean War.

Indianapolis Star,
Sunday, November 11, 1951

As the assault on Heartbreak Ridge entered its second week, September 20 saw relatively little ground action compared with the preceding seven days. With the line companies at low strength and many casualties yet to be evacuated, plans for that day were primarily for air strikes and artillery fires on the enemy.

From midnight until dawn the North Koreans made light but continual probing attacks against the Second (2/23) and Third (3/23) Battalions. In the morning hours B Company moving from the south and G

Company from the north launched a joint attack on Hill 931. Casualties from heavy enemy defensive fire—small arms, automatic weapons, mortar, and artillery—proved costly, so the two companies had to withdraw to their original positions by midafternoon.

Almost all of Third Battalion's wounded had been evacuated. K Company was now dug in, and an uneasy calm had settled over the weary troops. As so often in the past, Pfcs. Guy Robinson and Al Seghetti were sitting quietly in their foxhole while evening rations were being readied for distribution. Just then the acting platoon sergeant, Cliff Karlson, appeared over a ridgeline. Both Guy and Al stood up to face him, expectantly.

Sergeant Karlson called over to them, "Robinson . . . no, Seghetti, go up to the C.P. and get your rations."

Al responded immediately, climbing out of the foxhole. Guy watched his best friend disappear over the ridgeline. Guy gave no thought at the time as to why Karlson may have changed his mind about whom to send—he would think often about it later, though. Instead he was thinking how much he had come to like the outgoing, personable young man who was his own age, 21, and from the same state, Illinois, as he. (Guy was from Normal and Al from Peoria.)

Like himself, Al was of average size, maybe a little huskier, but, thought Guy, far better looking with his dark eyes and dark hair. They had been friends since joining K Company back in June, and were assigned together as a BAR team, Al as gunner and Guy as assistant gunner. Before going upon the line, the two had often spent their evenings trying to harmonize tunes without any accompanying music. One of their favorites was "I Only Have Eyes for You."

Unlike Guy, Al, who was a Catholic, talked openly about religion. When they were in especially dangerous situations, the friends would admit to each other how scared they really were. Just in the past few days Al had appeared even more apprehensive about his fate. Guy had heard him pray openly and heard him say several times, "God, I don't want to die."[1]

There had been only sporadic rounds of incoming mortar that day. While Al was picking up his and Guy's rations, a single round came in and exploded near the company command post. Guy got the word right away: "Al has been killed." His first thought was "Why Al? Why not me?" remembering that Sergeant Karlson had first called his name.

Guy did not go to see for himself, for he did not think that he could bear to look at his best friend's dead body. John Seybert saw the body and later told Guy that he could not understand why Al had died. There was no obvious fatal wound on his body that he could see, just a solitary shrapnel puncture on one leg.

One other man was killed by the same mortar round that had killed Al Seghetti. He was Sfc. Everett Ho, who had been first sergeant of Company K for only a few days.

The son and grandson of regular-army officers, James Yeates Adams was ideally suited to command those forces that had been given the mission of taking Heartbreak Ridge. A military professional in every way, he was indefatigable, determined, and tough but had an unsurpassed compassion for his men. Major Le Mire of the French Battalion in Korea has given a picturesque, but wholly accurate, description of this much-admired soldier: "Colonel Adams, very big, very slim, with the head of a bird of prey wherein eyes of great kindness generally repose."[2]

As a child Jim Adams spoke Chinese. The Asian continent held little mystery for him, for it was his birthplace. He was born on July 23, 1912, in Tientsin, China, where his father, Emory S. Adams, was serving as company commander of B Company in the old Fifteenth Infantry Regiment, once General Stilwell's outfit. The elder Adams was six feet two and one-half inches tall and weighed 230 to 240 pounds. Jim would eventually surpass (by three and one-half inches) his father in physical stature, if not in professional prominence, for Emory Adams would one day hold a most high military position: adjutant general of the United States Army.[3] Indeed, General Adams would be a lifelong inspiration and role model for his son, Jim. Yet one historian has described James Adams as a "brilliant but eccentric maverick, somewhat in the mold of Lawrence of Arabia."[4] This characterization may be apt if it is meant to describe him as an officer who did not hesitate to stand up to authority, placing his own reputation on line for what he thought right, especially when it concerned the welfare of his troops.

The second week of the assault on Heartbreak was such a time. Although suffering many casualties from U.S. artillery fire, the North Koreans had poured in fresh replacements. There were indications that the enemy had obtained a great increase in its own artillery ammunition and was firing artillery heavier than 120-mm. or 122-mm.

Somehow the enemy was able to identify vital centers in the Twenty-third's area and place accurate artillery fire upon them. In the morning of September 20, Third Battalion reported incoming artillery falling very close to their ammo dump in the Pia-ri Valley. At noon ten rounds of enemy 76s fell near the Twenty-third Regiment's forward command post, impacting in the bachelor officer quarters (BOQ) and staff tent area. Two hours later ten more rounds fell very close to the regimental forward command post.

The Twenty-third Infantry Regiment's troop strength, ammunition, medical supplies, and rations were all low. Believing his battalions were now in grave danger, Colonel Adams asked General de Shazo to be allowed to pull them off the line.

The acting commander, Second Division, relayed the situation to General Byers, the X Corps commanding general (CG), telling him that Adams "is getting in serious trouble." He presented the request, not as his own but as Adams's, that the Twenty-third be authorized to pull back. Byers replied, "I hate to see them withdraw, Tom."[5]

The corps commander then offered a C-119 drop the next day of ammo and rations. De Shazo informed Adams that no authority to pull back would be given. He told Adams, "My reputation is at stake. Your feet are to the fire. Go take that damn hill."[6]

There was nothing left for the colonel to do except try again, sending his men against a fanatical enemy entrenched on this formidable ridgeline. Jim Dick expressed the high regard that the men of the Twenty-third held for their regimental commander. "I would have gone up that hill armed with paper clips and rubber bands had Jim Adams told me to. I trusted Colonel Adams as a military commander more than anyone."[7]

The constant contact with the enemy and the helpless exposure to its maddening fires had gotten to one of the Twenty-third Battalion's commanders. When Colonel Adams made a frontline visit to Second Battalion, he found its commander taking refuge in a dugout. Adams tried to talk to him, but the battalion commander kept yelling, "Incoming, Incoming."

Instinctively, Adams dove into the hole also but soon discovered the realities of the situation. The battle-fatigued battalion commander simply couldn't distinguish incoming mortar from outgoing mortar. Colonel Adams relieved him on the spot and put Henry F. Daniels in as commanding officer. The big, handsome lieutenant colonel thereafter led the battered Second Battalion with distinction.

The hours spanning the night of the 20th and the early morning of September 21 were relatively quiet for the Twenty-third Infantry units. There were only sporadic enemy mortar and artillery fires falling upon them. Existing positions were maintained throughout the day, and resupply continued as the "choggy" bearers—the Korean laborers with their A-frames on their backs—struggled to bring their heavy loads up the rocky cliffs.

A coordinated attack by First and Second

Battalions (1/23 and 2/23) was planned against Hill 931 for the early morning of the 22nd. At 0545 hours First Battalion pushed up from the south while the Second Battalion moved down from the north. So fanatical was the enemy's defense of 931 that it called in mortar fire on its own positions. And so for U.S. forces to neutralize any one bunker, every North Korean defender in it first had to be killed.

Four times the First Battalion gained the top of the south knob of Hill 931, and four times they were driven off by heavy enemy mortar fire. Pfc. Willis Taylor, a BAR man in B Company, fired his weapon without letup, inflicting many casualties upon the enemy. During the North Korean counterattack, Taylor stubbornly held on to his hard-won position as his BAR continued to spew out deadly fire.

Earlier in the day a missile had hit Taylor's upper arm, but the wound was so superficial that the bullet could be removed on the spot by the medics. The next injury he received proved more serious, however. He was huddled in a hole with James Staggs from Pikeville, Kentucky, when enemy mortars moved in so close that the two men could hear the mortar rounds even as they came out of the tube. A round exploded near their hole, killing Staggs instantly. Several fragments went through Taylor's right ankle, fracturing the bones. He pulled another wounded man into the hole with him, and together they waited there for over an hour before being picked up by the medics.

On the north side E Company was knocking out one bunker at a time, making a slow advance over the rugged terrain. By 1700 hours E reached the base of

Hill 931's north knob. As enemy mortar and artillery fire intensified, the company had to pull back some 200 yards. There, both battalions established positions for the night. Out of the darkness the North Koreans struck time and time again, yet the men from their well-dug-in positions successfully repulsed them.

Third Battalion (3/23) remained in place that day but became the target of the inevitable mortar attack. With the loss of Al Seghetti, Guy Robinson had gained a new BAR teammate, Pfc. Delmar Burchette. Guy was now BAR gunner and Delmar assistant gunner. The two were sitting in their foxhole dug out of the rocky ground on the hillside when enemy mortar rounds started falling all around. Guy crouched down trying to make himself small underneath his steel pot as a mortar round came over, exploding nearby and scattering hot shrapnel like falling raindrops over Guy and Delmar's foxhole. Guy felt a sting on the back of his neck. Running his hand over his neck he found it covered with blood. Pieces of schrapnel had scattered around and underneath the rim of his steel helmet. Another piece had struck Guy in the left knee. When he looked up, he saw that Delmar, also, had been hit by several pieces of steel and that the side of his face and ear was covered in blood. After medics bandaged them up, Lieutenant Payne ordered them to be evacuated off Heartbreak Ridge.

Starting at 2115 hours the North Koreans began a series of platoon-size to company-size counterattacks against First and Second Battalion positions. Also, Third Battalion, during the night of September 22–23, repulsed repeated enemy attacks until daybreak.

Very early on Sunday morning, September 23, First Battalion launched an assault from the south against Hill 931 (see map 5). This first attack was repulsed; then there was a second attempt, also repulsed. The enemy defenders were throwing what appeared to be "sacksful of hand grenades" upon Master Sergeant Nicholas's First Platoon in A Company. At the same time they were firing their burp guns, the cheaply made Soviet 7.62-mm submachine guns. (Designed in World War II for volume rather than accuracy of fire, they held a 72-round magazine and could fire at a cyclic rate of 100 per minute.) Along with this barrage, North Korean machine-gun fire crisscrossed over A Company's positions. Right off eight or nine men of First Platoon were killed or seriously wounded.

While crouching back of a rocky ridge to reorganize for another attempt to take the unyielding hill, Nick Nicholas and his men decided among themselves that today would be the day. Talking over their situation, they concluded that this sorry affair would end only if they succeeded or all were killed in the attempt. Corporal Copeland from Lexington, Kentucky, expressed his own feelings and that of the others when he declared, "I'm tired of running up and down this hill. Let's go take it." Someone else added, "If we don't make it this time, we'll just be sent back again and again."[8]

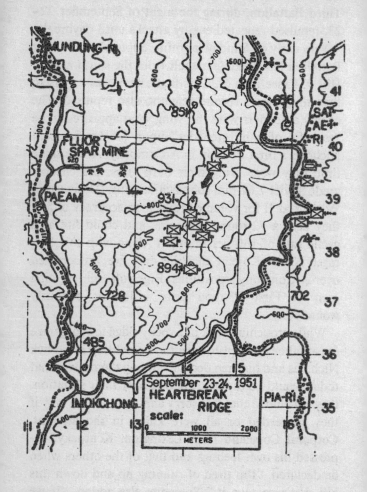

Map 5
Unit movements, September 23–24, 1951

The men fixed bayonets, prepared to drive out every last enemy soldier at the point of steel if there was no other way.

In his own mind Nick knew that time had run out for him. There had been too many close calls. He had been wounded by a hand grenade while at the Punchbowl and injured slightly by another one on Heartbreak on September 19. He felt calm now, resolved to accept his fate. While waiting for the jump-off, the lean sergeant lay looking out through a haze of misty rain. As the gray fog lifted that morning, he saw a squirrel running around out in no-man's-land. Back in Tennessee there were many gray squirrels as well as some red ones. But this squirrel was black, and Nick took it as a bad omen. Instinctively he wanted to shoot the creature. His index finger lay on his carbine's trigger, ready to squeeze off a round. Realizing that if he shot he might give away their position, Nick restrained himself.

When time came for the third attack, the men stood up to move in single file around the rocky ridge. Suddenly in front of them, not more than 20 to 30 feet away, appeared some enemy soldiers. One held a burp gun pointed right at Sergeant Nicholas.

There was no time to react, for the burp gun was firing full blast. Nick could see on a straight line in front of him little volcanic eruptions of dirt as the gun's flying bullets dug at intervals into the ground, coming every split second closer to him.

Instantly several bullets ripped into his body and Sergeant Nicholas crumpled to the ground. Even at that moment he kept control by grabbing hold of a little bush nearby and hanging on tenaciously; he might otherwise have rolled down the hill. And still he managed to fire at the enemy soldiers, emptying two of his carbine's magazines, which he had earlier taped together end to end. After that, all became a blur as he slipped in and out of unconsciousness.

Nick had at least nine holes in his body. He had been hit in the chest and the stomach, and some of the missiles had gone straight through his body, coming out the back. Several surgeries were required, and his grave injuries would plague him for years to come.

Captain Dick led Company A in two more attempts to take Hill 931 during the day of September 23, the fifth assault coming at 1750 hours in the evening. Eight hours earlier, at 0935, elements of First Battalion (1/23) had come within 150 yards of Hill 931's south knob. They were repulsed with mortar fire.

The hill had endured so much pounding from artillery and mortars from both U.S. troops and North Koreans that the once rocky ground they had to walk over was now pulverized dust. This made climbing the steep grade an added difficulty, for with each step the men's feet slipped on the fine powder. One rocky cliff had been so loosened by the incessant vibration from exploding shells that a huge boulder fragmented off, crashing down upon the 10 to 12 men taking refuge beneath it.

Hand grenades rained down upon them in such a heavy shower that Jim Dick thought it looked like apples pouring out of a bushel basket. When a hand grenade's fragment struck Dick in the calf of his left leg, he bandaged the wound to stop the bleeding but refused to be evacuated, for he was determined to lead A Company to the top of 931.

And he did just that. At least some of the company made it to the top. In the assault at 1750 three men using bayonets and hand grenades gained the crest of Hill 931. Reinforcements were sent up, and by 2000 hours 15 U.S. soldiers had clawed their way up the treacherous slopes to reach the final summit. They found the west slopes too rocky to dig in. There, so many enemy were dead that the bodies were stacked several high.

A Company's resolute commanding officer sustained a second injury that day. A small arms round cut through his fatigue shirt collar and grazed the back of his neck. As with his leg wound, he paid little attention to it, applying only a pressure bandage while going about directing his men in their movement up the hill.

The attack by Second Battalion (2/23) against Hill 931 from the north did not get under way until 1100 hours, having been delayed for ammunition supply depleted by the enemy probing attacks the night before. Their advance carried them to within yards of the hill's crest before they were stopped by artillery, mortar, automatic weapons, and small arms fire.

During the night of September 23–24, First Battalion (1/23) sent up more reinforcements to the little group on top of Hill 931 so that by 0130 hours there were about 40 men in all up there holding the hill's peak. It was then that screaming North Koreans, as many as a company, came rushing out of the darkness.

They poured in from the north and from the west, firing their burp guns and exploding hand grenades upon the defenders. At the same time mortar rounds came crashing in upon the fighting forces.

For two hours the hard-pressed men of First Battalion held out on top of Hill 931. All the while some 200–300 enemy troops were attacking the remainder of First Battalion units, so that the few survivors on 931 were in imminent danger of being surrounded. Their ammunition was running dangerously low. Nothing was left for them to do but to give up the prize they had won at such great cost and which they had tried so bravely to keep.

After the little group withdrew and linked up with the main body of the battalion, they fought with the others all the rest of that night to hold off the relentless attacks by the enemy. Captain Dick's diary entry of A Company's action reads as follows:

23 Sept.—Able attacks 931 at 0330 hrs. Lt. Meiner LWIA. Lt. Gregory SWIA, Sgt. Nicholas SWIA, Co. Cmdr. WIA twice. Too many other MIA, KIA, WIA to record. Six assaults and finally made it to the top. Could not hold against counterattack, as there were only 20 officers and men left on the hill from Able, Baker, and Charlie. [Dick's abbreviations: WIA, wounded in action; L, lightly; S, seriously; MIA, missing in action; KIA, killed in action.]

Le Mire, the French soldier-historian, summarized the results of the combat for that period:

There is nothing left of the wooded ridge. Some skeletons of pines break up under the last shells' burst. Clouds of dust rise out of the upturned earth. Blocks of rocks jut into the air. The general form of the summit of 931 can no longer be recognized. An area 300 meters long and 100 meters wide has already been dug up by more than 100,000 cannon rounds. The aspect of the battle is fantastic. Our firing mixes with that of the enemy without a break. Sheets of projectiles sail through the sky in bursts of deafening noise, coming from our side as well as from the other side. One can no longer tell who is firing, if it is our artillery that supports us or the enemy firing back.

And yet, in the middle of this crushing of iron and bursting of rocks, the First Battalion, until 1900 hours, section by section, group by group renews its attempts. Three men from here, from there, without orders, jump forward to try to take foot and to permit the battalion to attain its objective at whatever cost, just to finish it, so that the nightmare ends. All bloody, the First Battalion is like a mortally wounded wolf who does not want to allow himself to be taken.

At twilight, eight fighter-bombers attack 931 with bombs, rockets and heavy machine-gun fire. They plunge, disappear behind the ridges, climb again and come back like furious bumblebees. The First Battalion is exhausted, its sacrifice cannot last any longer. It receives the order to pull back on the slopes. In spite of its heroism it cannot take the second bastion of Heartbreak. Night falls on the dead already entombed under the shattered branches and the upturned earth.[9]

Another contemporary writer, a U.S. lieutenant by the name of Clark C. Munroe, summed it up much in the same way: "While in the valley below, the trees turned autumn golden and red and leaves littered the ground much as they did back home, on the hills there was only the pock-marked hard and dusty earth littered with steel and blood and the remains of men who had given all they possessed."[10]

Throughout the whole of the next day the already battered battalion endured enemy mortar, machine-gun, and small arms fire.

Back at the division command post near Yanggu the usually tough, hard-bitten assistant division commander was agonizing over assigning newly arrived second lieutenants as company replacements. He personally met all new arrivals and tried to give them some understanding about what lay ahead for them.

Brig. Gen. Haydon L. Boatner, "The Bull," had graduated number one in his West Point class of 1924. His Asian service went back to 1928, to Tientsin, China, where he served with the mounted scouts of the old Fifteenth Infantry Regiment. He was fluent in Mandarin (Middle Kingdom Chinese).

A little over a decade later, in 1942, found him in Burma serving with the legendary Lt. Gen. Joseph W. "Vinegar Joe" Stilwell. Boatner on one occasion filled a role as his chief's personal representative to President Roosevelt and so ingratiated himself with his commander-in-chief that he was able to persuade the personable president to send a radiogram to Winston

Churchill urging better cooperation with Stilwell by the British in India.[11]

Peering out of cold, pale eyes behind round wire-rimmed glasses set atop a hooked nose, The Bull could spit out such caustic words in his high-pitched voice that senior officers on the receiving end likened it to a chewing out by the colorful General George S. Patton, Jr. But beneath that crusty outer shell, deep emotions stirred. The tough general had a special feeling for young officers. After all, wouldn't his own son, 2d Lt. James G. Boatner, soon be coming to Korea?

The feeling was intense. Upon each one of these smooth-faced young men he sent to a frontline unit, felt the general, he had proclaimed a sentence of death.[12]

For many of them, it was just that.

At 0830 hours on September 24, the Second Battalion (2/23) jumped off with G Company in the lead to make yet another attack, this one from the north, against Hill 931. Throughout the day's assaults the enemy remained stubborn, its impregnable bunkers supporting each other. Withering fire from enemy mortar and artillery rained down upon the attackers. Enemy machine-gun and small arms fire ripped through their ranks as the men of Second Battalion attempted, unsuccessfully, to scale the steep northern approach to 931. At dusk they halted.

Sometimes life or death may be decided by the mere crook of a finger, as it was for Joe Melton. Joe Melton, from Denton, Texas, was an ammo bearer in H Company, Second Battalion, Twenty-third Infantry

Regiment. The usual employment of a heavy weapons company is to attach one machine-gun squad to each of the battalion's three rifle companies for added fire support. So it happened that Joe and two other men found themselves attached to G Company manning a heavy .30-caliber, water-cooled machine gun.

Their position was on the crest of a rocky ridge, so rocky that they couldn't dig in, not one inch. Immediately behind them was a sharp drop off, straight down, some 200 feet.

When the attack began on September 24, Joe's crew started firing. In short order they expended two boxes of .30-caliber ammunition. The machine gun's flash and constant rattle drew the enemy's attention and, inevitably, incoming mortar. The ground beneath them shook as a mortar round exploded less than 20 yards in front of their exposed position. A second round roared instantly over their heads to drop off behind them and roll harmlessly down the steep cliff. It was simply a matter of zeroing in: one round in front of the target, one round behind the target, and the third—bull's-eye.

For the three young men, no hope remained. They were just as helpless as ants on a hill, about to be stepped upon. All they could do was press their bodies against the hard ground as close as they could, which wasn't much. The ground was solid rock.

They prayed as the round came in. It impacted with a thundering jolt right in front, spraying shrapnel and dirt in a thick cloud all over their bodies.

One by one the men looked up, wiping the dirt and grime out of their eyes. "You okay?"

"Yeah, you?"

Unbelievably not one of the three had received a scratch.

They surveyed the damage. All their ammunition had exploded. Mortar shrapnel had split the machine gun's water jacket wide open, so that it would be impossible to fire the weapon anymore. The machine-gun crew was thus effectively out of commission. They just stayed where they were until the attack ended at about 1700 hours. Then they started cleaning up the debris.

Joe looked up to see Lieutenant Pillsbury beckoning to him with a crook of his finger. "Melton, come here."

He walked over to stand in front of his platoon leader. "Pick somebody to go with you and take that gun back to be repaired by Ordnance."

The sun had dipped behind the last ragged peak, and it would soon be dark. Joe didn't like the idea of going three miles through mine fields, through enemy-infested territory, to carry the nearly destroyed gun all the way back to H Company. Besides, he already had a good foxhole dug and was ready to share it that night with Pfc. Hollis Creasy, a 21-year-old from Sardis, Tennessee.

But he entertained no thought of not obeying an order from an officer. Joe Melton always did what he was told to do no matter what the consequences might be. He picked Norman Owyang to go with him.

The two ran, one carrying the gun and the other the tripod, trying not to think about the mines and their ensnaring wires. Mostly they slipped and slid down the mountainside on their butts, for rain had made the ground slippery. Arriving in record time, they reported to H Company's commander, Lt. Ira L. Simmerling, a big hulking man who towered over them. They were relieved to hear him order, "You two spend the night here. No need to go back up there until morning."

So it was that crook of Lt. Pillsbury's finger that decided Joe's fate. For that night a single enemy mortar round came in, scoring a direct hit on the foxhole back at G Company and instantly killing Pfc. Hollis Creasy—as well as the man who had been put there to share it in Joe Melton's place.[13]

Another man, Pfc. Harlan C. King from Bennett, Nebraska, considered himself very lucky also. A few days before, he had been sitting with two other C Company men, in a bunker. They were feeling uneasy and decided to go over a little way to join their squad leader, Sgt. Raul Mendoza. A single mortar round came in. Looking back they saw the bunker they had just left completely demolished.

Now with a leg injury Pfc. Harlan King was walking off Heartbreak Ridge. While crouching in a shallow hole, pinned down by enemy machine-gun fire, he had been struck by bullet fragments ricocheting off a rock. A few small fragments struck him in the face while two other pieces of metal lodged in his left thigh. Despite his wounds King carried on his back one of his comrades who had leg injuries more serious than his own. After two to three weeks in a hospital, King returned to combat.

In the early morning hours of September 25, beginning at 0130, an estimated enemy platoon made a probing attack on B Company (1/23) positions. After one and one-half hours, friendly defensive fire succeeded in driving off the penetrating force.

The three battalions, 1/23, 2/23, and 3/23, remained in defensive positions all day in order to reorganize, and all the time they were harassed by sporadic incoming mortar and artillery fire and by enemy sniper fire. Their positions were such that the enemy could observe them directly, particularly the First Battalion. Any time a man moved from his foxhole, a hail of enemy fire poured down upon him.

6

Bataillon Français de l'O.N.U.: The French Battalion of the United Nations

Very few combat units in the course of history can boast of as many feats of arms.

Robert N. Young
Major General, Commander,
Second Infantry
Division[1]

Flying the tricolor blue, white, and red flag of the Fourth Republic, the dark troop ship SS *Athos II* slid through Pusan Harbor's black waters.

Thirty-five days' sail out of Marseilles on the Gulf of Lyons (France's chief southern seaport since the fifteenth century), lying beneath blue and sunny Mediterranean skies, the vessel carried 1,043 combat troops, all volunteers. Arriving in Pusan Harbor the morning of November 29, the vessel that day put ashore supplies and equipment. The troops slept a last night on shipboard and began disembarking early on the morning of the 30th. While the French Battalion spent its last hours on the *Athos II,* Chinese "volunteers" came pouring across the Yalu River into frozen, snowblanketed North Korea to enter the fight against U.N. forces.

Whatever the relationship between the two governments of France and the United States—sometimes cordial, sometimes strained—cooperation between the French and U.S. military has been unprecedented in the affairs of nations. The Marquis de Lafayette stood with them when the American colonies became assured of their independence by the surrender of the British at Yorktown in October 1781. For five years preceding that final event the great French general had served invaluably as confidant and trusted ally to the revolutionary leader Gen. George Washington and his fledgling army of citizen-soldiers. One hundred thirty-six years later, Gen. John J. Pershing and the American Expeditionary Force (AEF) were in France— "Lafayette, we are here"[2]—helping the French defeat the Kaiser's army.

French freedom fighters and U.S. soldiers joined together in the 1940s on the European continent to defeat Nazi Germany, and many times French soldier and U.S. soldier stood shoulder to shoulder on the battlefield, sharing hardships and ideals as only fighting men can know them, even though they came from different cultural backgrounds.

Although the French Army had just come through nearly six years of bitter struggle for its homeland, for the planned invasion of Japan, the French government offered to provide the U.S. command an army corps of two infantry divisions, plus service and supporting units.[3] Use of the atomic bomb and the early surrender of Japan rendered the plan unnecessary, however.

Five years after, when a new and different threat appeared in this part of Asia and the United Nations issued a call for "members to give Korea such help as might be needed to repel the armed attack and to restore peace in the area,"[4] France again made a ready response although she was already heavily engaged militarily in Indochina.

On July 22, 1950, the government of René Pleven determined to aid in repelling North Korean aggression. It ordered the immediate dispatch of the frigate *La Grandiere,* then a part of the French Far Eastern naval forces operating in Indo-Chinese waters, which was to proceed toward the Sea of Japan. Upon arrival there, the vessel would be placed at the disposal of the U.N. naval forces.

About a month later the French government decided to commit an independent battalion, designated Premier Battalion Français de l' O.N.U.—the First French Battalion of the United Nations. This name was sometimes shortened to Boeuf O.N.U.

Within a week, Camp d'Auvours, in the western French department of Sarthe, bustled with activity as the organization and training of the French force got under way. From all parts of France, coming from the active army and from the reserves, volunteers arrived, determined to fight in Korea. Some were paratroopers, and some, like their soon-to-be-designated commander, were from the French foreign legion.

On September 18 France's secretary of war, designated Gen. de Corps d'Armee Magrin Vernerrey, better known to U.S. forces as Lt. Gen. Ralph Monclar, as commander of the French forces. Monclar, an illustrious figure in the annals of the French military and World War II protegé of Gen. Charles de Gaulle, would lend color to the French Battalion in Korea. He would also be the subject of much speculation.

An oft-repeated rumor was that Monclar accepted a reduction of rank from general to lieutenant colonel in order to lead the French Battalion. The fact is that he continued to hold the rank and receive the pay of general in the French army while assenting to replace only his general's four stars[5] with a lieutenant colonel's five gold and silver bars. There were occasions when Monclar wore his general's uniform in Korea, and even those U.S. colonels under whose command he served called him general.

The appointment of a general to head a battalion-size force did not alone lead to the confusion that was to involve the French command structure. Monclar had his own staff of 7 senior officers and 27 enlisted men that constituted a kind of super-headquarters above that of the battalion headquarters. It always accompanied and remained physically located with the combat battalion, often interjecting itself into the operational control of the battalion. Two theories have been advanced to explain why this super-headquarters came to be: One is that the military expected that the French government would eventually authorize a division for Korea. The other theory is that this was an opportunity for these senior French officers to observe firsthand for their own edification the combat operations.

Recognizing that the U.S. command would be in overall control of the combat units in Korea, the French organized their battalion along the lines of a standard U.S. infantry battalion. At full strength, the battalion contained 39 officers, 172 noncommissioned officers, and 806 privates, including combat service personnel of 10 officers, 40 noncommissioned officers, and 150 privates.

Training of the battalion took place at Camp d'Auvours from the time of the battalion's organization on September 1 until October 25, when the troops embarked at the port of Marseilles on the SS *Athos II,* an old German liner that the French had taken over after World War I and converted for troop transport. Camp d'Auvours continued as a permanent training site for the first year of the Korean War for the organization and training of future reinforcement detachments. These detachments were phased to arrive in Korea every two months to replace the expected casualty losses of the battalion.

To prepare for the arrival of the main body of French troops, an advance party of four French Army officers flew to Korea in August. The party was headed by Lt. Col. Guy de Cockborne, Monclar's chief of staff, who had recently been a battalion commander in the French foreign legion in Indochina.

De Cockborne, of sturdy build and with heavy, deep-cut facial lines reflecting his Scottish ancestry,[6] was by nature methodical and thorough, characteristics that ideally suited him for staff work. Accompanying him were a quartermaster officer, a medical officer, Lieutenant Colonel Brunel, and an armor officer, Capt. Louis-Christian Michelet. Captain Michelet had an impressive background in U.S. military schools as a graduate (1949) of the Command and General Staff College at Fort Leavenworth and of the Ordnance Officer's Advance Course at Aberdeen Proving Ground. He was also fluent in English.

The four officers flew by commercial airline from Paris to Tokyo and then on to Pusan, Korea. Leaving the doctor and the quartermaster officer behind in Pusan, de Cockborne and Michelet flew to Seoul and eventually wound up far to the north on the Chongchon River, where the Second U.S. Division was located.

Arriving at the Chongchon River, the French liaison officers felt the full impact of North Korea's bitter cold as they made contact with U.S. commanders and staff officers to coordinate organization and supply in preparation for the French Battalion's planned attachment to the Second Division. They then hurried back to Pusan to see the French Battalion land at the end of November.

The troop train's cars were filled to overflowing as the newly arrived battalion traveled by rail to the U.N. reception center in Taegu. There, new weapons and supplies were issued, including arctic shoes. Even though no one in the battalion had ever seen two of these weapons—the recoilless rifle, 57, and the recoilless rifle, 75—soon they would employ them with great effectiveness.

An urgent call came from Tokyo: General Monclar had arrived and was calling for an escort to Korea. So de Cockborne left to accompany him to Seoul.

An intense and highly conscientious officer, Captain Michelet believed his in-depth knowledge of the U.S. military could help smooth the integration of the French Battalion with the U.S. Army. Quite unlike what is seen in the U.S. Army, Michelet spoke with unusual candor for an officer of lower rank speaking to a general when he sought to advise Monclar about the differences in U.S. and French military structure and functioning. Once he accompanied the general to a meeting with a U.S. inspector general. Michelet attempted to brief Monclar about the inspector general's role in the U.S. Army, which he understood to be different from that in the French army. Monclar brushed the captain aside, declaring, "I know all there is to know about inspector generals. I was inspector general of the French foreign legion."[7] Michelet frequently found his translation tasks frustrating.

After an 11-day stay in Taegu the French Battalion moved to Suwon, just south of Seoul. There it became attached to the Second U.S. Division's Twenty-third Infantry Regiment, under the command of Col. Paul L. Freeman. The Second Division had pulled back to Suwon following its near-disastrous encounter with Chinese "volunteers" on the Chongchon. Thereafter, the French took part in all the Indianhead Division's engagements with the enemy.

In January 1951 the fierce battle of Wonju took place, during which, on the seventh day, the French Battalion suffered its first casualty from enemy action. (One French soldier had been killed previously by the collapse of a bunker around Christmastime.)

Another hard-fought battle—Twin Tunnels—took place on February 1 and 2. Enemy fire killed Lt. Ange Nicolai of the Third Company and Capt. André Le Maitre, the heavy weapons company commander. The action at Twin Tunnels won for the French Battalion its first U.S. presidential citation and the unit citation of the French army.

Other equally violent engagements followed: Chipyong-ni from February 3 to February 16, and the assault on Hill 1037, an exclusively French action, from March 3 to March 5. Badly mauled, the French Battalion suffered 40 killed and 200 wounded. Then came the Chinese communist spring offensive, the May Massacre, and at the end of August, Bloody Ridge.

While the three U.S. infantry battalions of Colonel Adams's Twenty-third Infantry Regiment (1/23, 2/23, and 3/23) were making repeated direct assaults, beginning September 13, against the 851, 931, and 894 hill mass, the French Battalion played a significant supporting role in the Satae-ri Valley and against the hills forming the high ground to the east of that valley. Its mission was to keep the North Koreans bottled up on the Watch Dog—that is, Hill 656, which "splits the narrow valley like a prow"[8]—to prevent them from coming down into the back of the U.S. troops.

For this operation Commandant Merle de Beaufond was in direct command of the French Battalion. Oliver Le Mire, the bespectacled commandant who had commanded the battalion since its inception almost a year earlier, had now moved up to the general staff of Monclar. Commandant Maurice L. Barthélémy served as de Beaufond's deputy and second in command. Five companies made up the battalion: the three infantry companies First, Second and Third; the C.A. Company, which contained a section of 75-mm Recoilless rifles, a .50-caliber machine-gun section, and a section of 81-mm mortars; and the C.C.B., the supply and service company, which also contained a platoon of pioneers. The code names for the three rifle companies were, respectively, Xavier, Yvonne, and Zoé. The French Battalion itself carried the code designation Icicle.

On September 13 the French Battalion was positioned with its First and Second Companies on Hill 868, located 2,100 meters northeast of Pia-ri and a little over 1,000 meters due east of Satae-ri Valley, while the Third Company was in reserve, 1,200 meters to the rear in the direction of Pia-ri on Hill 754.

At 1600 hours on September 14 the battalion received the order to occupy Hill 841, 800 meters to its front, in order to attack Hill 1052 on the next day. Hill 1052 lay an additional 800 meters to the northeast. At 1645 hours First Company, led by Captain Tikhodoumoff, moved out. As night came on, the company formed a perimeter defense at the foot of 841.

The order to attack 1052 arrived at the units just at midnight. First and Third Companies led the assault, which began at 0700. The North Koreans fought hard, putting up a stiff resistance, so that immediately the French lost 15 men, including one of their officers. The French then called for artillery. For a full two and one-half hours, instead of the usual 30-minute artillery preparation, shells thundered overhead and pounded down upon 841 and 1052. First Company resumed its attack and came within 15 meters of 1052's crest. From well-camouflaged blockhouses the North Korean defenders poured out upon the attackers a blanket of grenades. To the French the blockhouses appeared mostly untouched despite the earlier heavy artillery bombardment. At 1700 hours First and Third Companies were ordered to withdraw. In all, they had suffered 30 wounded, including 3 officers and 3 noncommissioned officers.

The attempts to take Hills 841 and 1052 were called off to await the taking by the Republic of Korea troops (ROK) of Hill 1211, located 1,100 meters to the northeast of 1052. Meanwhile, C.A. Company kept up an active fire with its 75-mm recoilless rifles and 81-mm mortars upon the enemy installations on 841 and 1052 in order to help protect the U.S. soldiers assaulting Heartbreak Ridge.

On September 17 the Fifth ROK in regimental strength struck at 1211. After fierce fighting on that hillside the ROKs withdrew in the evening. During the night of September 20 they again seized 1211 but lost it to the North Koreans. The next day the French observed a relief column of several hundred North Koreans climbing toward 1052 and 1211. Once more, on September 22, the Fifth ROK took 1211 but was pushed off by an enemy night counterattack. The next day, also, the ROKs retook and relost 1211.

The French Battalion then received an order to shift its effort from the eastern high ground to the Heartbreak Ridge central hill mass. The order, which came on September 24, instructed the Battalion to replace on the next day the Second Battalion of the Twenty-third Regiment (2/23) in its positions north of Hill 931. The plan was for the 2/23 to move south and replace the battered First Battalion (1/23) on the southern slopes of 931. However, before the exchange of battalions could take place, the French Battalion (Fr/23) and the First Battalion (1/23) would coordinate in a determined assault against 931.

Relationship between First Battalion's Company A and the French Battalion had always been good. On the afternoon before July 4, Independence Day, for example, G.I.s of Company A and their French comrades had played a spirited game of volleyball. That evening, officers of Company A were guests of the French Battalion officers for dinner. Company A's captain, Jim Dick, a military man in the making since his early youth, greatly admired Commandant Barthélémy, the deputy commander of the French Battalion. After going on a personal reconnaissance with the French officer, Jim Dick remarked: "Trying to stay up with Major Barthélémy is like walking alongside a running deer. He never stops for a rest and he never seems to require water."[9]

The Third Company, commanded by Lieutenant L'Heritier, was the first of the two companies, Yvonne and Zoé, to reach its new positions north of Hill 931. On that September day, even before the night set in, an unrelenting barrage of enemy mortars fell upon them. The lieutenant adjutant and 20 men were wounded, and two noncommissioned officers, Sergeant Mare Hubert and Joseph Falconetti, were killed.

Strikingly like the U.S. Twenty-third Regiment's Company A in which Captain Dick, an officer, and Sergeant First Class Rothenberg, an enlisted man, formed a lasting comradeship on Heartbreak Ridge, two men in the French Third Company began a close friendship in Korea that would continue throughout their lives, although their appearances as soldiers were quite different. Second Lieutenant Pierre Collard, tall, erect, and always with an immaculately groomed mustache, presented a sharp contrast to his enlisted friend, Jean-Louis Posiere. Posiere, a former paratrooper, wearing G.I. combat boots and loosely fitting fatigue pants and jacket, while slouched beside a field tent could have been mistaken for any American "dog face." Although they took part in many hard-fought battles that first year of the Korean War, Collard and Posiere would survive them all, including Heartbreak Ridge, to return to their native France.

The Second Company, Yvonne, did not reach its new positions until early in the morning of September

26. The night relief had taken place under a hail of enemy artillery shells and enfilading machine-gun fire. The shelling constantly cut their telephone wires. Captain Robert Goupil, with straight nose, wavy dark hair, and sparkling eyes, epitomized the image that the French expected of an officer. With all sincerity his men called him the "Archangel."[10]

Goupil entered St. Cyr, the West Point of France, in 1939 at the age of 18. Leaving military school as a sublieutenant in the spring of 1941, he went immediately to Indochina. There, given command of a border post, he sustained serious injuries while fighting the Japanese invaders. The young officer continued fighting in Indochina and Laos until he returned to France in August 1946. With the Asian war still going on, upon his own request Goupil went again to Saigon. This was in June 1947. After 32 additional months of duty there, he returned the next time to his homeland in March 1950. When the Korean War broke out the adventurous soldier volunteered for BOEF O.N.U.

Within their battalion the French formed a company of Koreans. Because Captain Goupil had had much previous experience with Asians during his long service in Indochina, he was naturally given command of this company. These Koreans under Goupil's leadership fought gallantly in most of the fierce battles that took place in the winter and spring of 1951. Then on June 14 Captain Goupil took over command of Second Company.

Arriving at their designated positions on a partially wooded ridge separated from 931 by a little knob, Second Company prepared to go into the attack. Just as Lieutenant Moissinac-Massenat heard Goupil say, "Okay. We go," mortars began to fall. Commandant Beaufond, the battalion commander, radioed the company to speak to Yvonne-6.

Goupil responded, "Je grimpe sur la crete dix métres plus haut pour mieux voir." (I'm going to climb ten meters farther up the ridge to see better.)

Then there was silence. Beaufond called out loudly, "Donnez moi Yvonne en personne." (Give me Yvonne in person.) But Yvonne did not respond anymore.

After several seconds another person took over the radio transmission. Finally a strangled voice revealed, "Yvonne vient d'être tué." (Yvonne was just killed.)[11]

Lieutenant Moissinac-Massenat had been crouching in a shell hole just two to three meters to the left of Captain Goupil when the mortars began exploding. He felt the concussion and saw the company commander and his radio operator both killed. Just outside of Massenat's hole was another man, yelling, "I am wounded, I am wounded." Massenat pulled the man into the shell hole with him and applied pressure bandages to his bleeding wounds.

Goupil's comrades recovered his body and laid it out in a field tent. Then they took turns coming up to the tent entrance and rendering a military salute in final respect for their fallen company commander. Ironically, the officer who came up to take over command of Second Company, Lieutenant Barre, had been placed under arrest by Captain Goupil just the day before for arguing with a superior officer.

Preceded by an artillery preparation of 105s and

155s for 20 minutes, and a heavy air strike to the south and the west of 931, Third Company unleashed its assault at 1430 hours. One section of Third Company moved up by the east slopes of 931 and another by the west. Enemy mortars, grenades, and automatic weapons tied the section in the west to the ground so that it soon lost 50 percent of its effectiveness. It was passed by one platoon of Second Company, which got to within 30 meters of its objective but also became tied down by enemy fire from the blockhouses. At 1700 hours, after losing more than 100 men, Third Company was authorized to pull back on its base of departure in order to resupply.

After the First Battalion (1/23) had supported from the south the French Battalion's efforts of September 26 to take Hill 931, the Second Battalion (2/23) relieved First Battalion the next day.

PART
II

SECOND PHASE

7

A New Coach, a New Play

> Although Bob has been in college four years he has never learned the meaning of the word "quit." He has always been a hard fighter and a leader. The class has always looked to him when it wanted to "put something across."
>
> *Class of '22 resume of Robert N. Young,*
> *University of Maryland, "Terra Mariae" Yearbook*

Many times during the last days of September a lone engine's drone and the whir of a small airplane's prop attracted the attention of frontline troops in their foxholes on Heartbreak Ridge. Looking up, they saw a curious aircraft with a single-brace high wing—an L-19. The plane carried Maj. Gen. Robert Young, the new commander of the Second Infantry Division.

Just 14 days into the twentieth century had marked the birth, in Washington, D.C., of Robert Nichols

Young. In June of 1922, a month after he graduated with a Bachelor of Arts degree from the University of Maryland, Robert Young received a commission as a second lieutenant in the infantry reserve, and then in the regular army, six months later.

During World War II Young had assignments at various times as secretary of the War Department general staff, assistant division commander (ADC) of the Seventieth Infantry Division, Fort Lewis, Washington, and as acting ADC and ADC of the Third Infantry Division in the European theater of operations from October 1944 to July 1945. Although General Young had been wounded in January 1945 and had received, in addition to the Purple Heart, the Silver Star for gallantry in action, he had never commanded a unit in battle. His assignment to Korea as Commanding General, Second Infantry Division, was Robert Nichols Young's first combat command.

Second Infantry Division's new commander, wearing two bright stars of a major general for only four days, arrived at the division command post, near Yanggu in the afternoon of September 19. Brigadier General de Shazo, acting commander since September 1, had been slated to leave upon Young's arrival, but typical of top-level army bureaucracy, a foul-up occurred so that the orders transferring the general were delayed for several days. While Young familiarized himself with his new command, de Shazo remained on, directing operations very much as he had done for the past 19 days. Contact with the enemy on Heartbreak continued.

General Young began making his own assessment of

112

the existing situation on Heartbreak Ridge, which he knew had already cost the division so many casualties. He made several reconnaissance flights in his L-19, crisscrossing the frontline battle positions, studying the rugged terrain from many different angles. He had been told that the terrain would not permit tank movement across it, but the general wanted to see for himself.

Just as soon as General Young took full control, Colonel Adams made his resolve: Without success he had tried his best to get Brigadier General de Shazo to call off these suicidal piecemeal attacks, but now he must try again. This time he planned to get support in his efforts. The Twenty-third Regiment's commander telephoned down to the French Battalion.

Later in the evening, General Monclar and Commandant Le Mire called at the command post tent of Colonel Adams, as he had requested them to do. The thin, tall colonel, who had to duck down to go through the tent's entrance flap, greeted them. After they were all seated on folding field chairs, Adams opened the conversation.

"You are now the longest-serving Second Division soldiers in Korea. Tell me what you think about this attack. How do you think we ought to take the Heartbreak line?"

Monclar thought only briefly before speaking. "It will first be necessary to get around the Heartbreak mountain mass by way of the Mundung-ni Valley. In this way we will cut the enemy's maneuver and supply lines."

A grim Adams listened attentively to Monclar's

words. The respected French general was expressing Adam's own thoughts on the matter.

"Then, when this envelopment from the west reaches 931, we will coordinate attacks against 931 and 851 from the west and east simultaneously."

The U.S. colonel said not a word. He simply reached for his field telephone.

"Get me General Young.

"General, this is Jim Adams."

The two French guests in the colonel's tent remained silent, yet they could not hear what was being said on the other end of the line. They did hear Adams say, "Perhaps, General, you think that for the last 15 days we have been fighting some sheep herders on these hills. Well, that's not so. These North Koreans are tough. They are not easy to dislodge. If we continue the way we are going, in another week there will be no more Twenty-third Regiment."

Talking rapidly, the colonel hardly caught his breath. "You know what the French think? They say that the division must attack first by the Mundung-ni Valley; otherwise, we will never succeed. It is a mistake to attack by the interior."

There was silence. In a moment, as Adams hung up the phone, an audible sigh escaped his lips.

Wearily he reached for a bottle of Kentucky bourbon. "Very well," he began, balancing the whiskey bottle on his knee, "the general will be here tomorrow morning. We will tell him our little story. He will listen to us."[1] Colonel Adams poured a drink for his two guests and himself.

The next morning Monclar played the role of gracious host to General Young. Wearing a short-sleeved khaki uniform and a beret cocked on the side of his head, the French general went out to greet the Second Division commander. With a .45-caliber pistol slung on his right hip, Monclar walked sprightly, carrying a crooked-handled cane over one arm.

When the two men arrived at the French Battalion headquarters, an unusual sight greeted the American general's eyes. Here in this rugged combat setting stood a long table covered with a white linen tablecloth. Bottles of French champagne and stemmed crystal wine glasses were set on the table.

Monclar directed General Young to sit on one side at the table's head, and Colonel Adams sat down at his commander's left. While Young sipped champagne, his French host stood across from him on the other side of the table and presented his plan. As he talked, Monclar frequently pointed to terrain maps held by Colonel de Cockborne. With short-cropped gray hair, rimmed glasses, and a cigarette stub clenched between his teeth as his lower jaw jutted forward, the French general presented an image that might have been portrayed by the actor Spencer Tracy.

Forcefully Monclar argued that the Mundung-ni Valley was the key to defeating the North Koreans on Heartbreak Ridge. A drive up the valley would disrupt the enemy's supply and maneuver lines.

Colonel Adams summed it up: "To continue as we have been doing is suicide."

General Ridgway would later single out this stand of James Adams as an example of the highest moral courage. Said Ridgway in later years: "For a field commander to express it to his superior takes high moral courage, the sort of courage I have always felt is more important in a commander even than physical courage. Physical courage is never in short supply in a fighting army. Moral courage sometimes is."[2]

General Young bought the idea of broadening the attack and, in turn, sold it to General Byers, the X Corps commander. The piecemeal attacks were called off, though some fire fights with the enemy took place.

All of the Twenty-third's battalions received harassing mortar and artillery fire on September 27, which continued on the 28th as well. Under gray skies and in drizzly rain, on the next day First Battalion relieved Third Battalion in its positions. Third Battalion then moved to an assembly area. The enemy tried to impede this relief with heavy small arms and machine-gun fire from the ridge leading off Hill 851.

On October 1, the Second Division staff gathered in the command post tent for a briefing. Present were Lt. Cols. Albert Aykrod, G-2, and Arthur Cornelson, G-4; Majs. Daniel Hughes, G-1, and Thomas Mellon, G-3; and Col. Edwin "Ted" Walker, Divarty commander. After hearing individual briefings by each staff member, General Young stood up to address the group as follows:

I want to outline what my thinking is for an operation with a target date for later in the week. So far we have been going after one hill after another. We have the mission of eventually getting up to the Hays line, and the enemy has so far been able to concentrate his mortars on hill after hill. It seems to me it would be smart to run an operation in which we close to the line in a hurry with many attacks going on at once—all on the objective at once. Then he'll have to disperse his mortar fires.

The division commander pointed out how the Ninth Infantry should go up the left boundary of the division zone to take a succession of objectives, while the Thirty-eighth Infantry was to go up the sector's center to seize other hills lying to the west of Mundung-ni Valley, and the four battalions of the Twenty-third, attacking simultaneously, would gain Hills 851, 931, and 728, which he called the "key terrain feature in the whole area . . . almost equal in importance to 931." Young then continued:

The regimental COs are enthusiastic. The corps commander approves. The road situation for the first part of the operation may be difficult. It means the stocking of supplies now so as to be ahead of the game. Possibly, Friday will put us on the Hays line. Except for the necessary flank security, we can hold that line with fewer forces than we are using now. I call it Operation Touchdown.

General Young said he wanted a tank-infantry operation to go to Mundung-ni, and that the tanks were to stay up on line all night to protect the infantry. He directed the engineers to accompany the tanks and concluded, "It must be a bold movement—even if we lose tanks they'll have earned their keep."[3]

Even before General Young made the formal announcement of Operation Touchdown, the division staff officers were able to start their planning. They had been alerted on the evening before, September 30, about the proposed operation. The target date, set for October 5, gave them five days to get ready.

The time allowed to prepare was none too long. Lieutenant Colonel Cornelson, G-4, had several problems facing him as he began work on the logistic plan. The projected daily expenditure of artillery ammunition (16,000 rounds of 105-mm ammo and 4,000 of 155-mm ammo) made up the bulk of the division's 1,200 tons of supply that needed to be moved forward each day. The division's organic transportation was not adequate to carry this large amount.

Since the Mundung-ni Valley would take the key tank-infantry push, and all the division's artillery battalions were to be positioned in the western half of Second Division's zone, the main supply effort had to be devoted to that area. But here the terrain presented a major difficulty. A defile separated the frontline units from the existing supply dumps and could be traversed only over five miles of a one-way stretch of road on an 8 percent grade. There was always the possibility that enemy artillery fire could close the defile.

By Tuesday, October 2, Lieutenant Colonel Cornelson had the logistical portion of the operation order virtually complete. He planned to establish an ammunition supply point (ASP) and emergency Class I and III supply dumps in the west valley. In the evening of October 3, the ASP, named Ivanhoe Surge

Point, was set up in the vicinity of Pol-mal, which lay in the Mundung-ni Valley a little over eight miles southwest of Heartbreak Ridge. Men from 702d Ordnance Company and Division Artillery, together with some Korean laborers, formed an improvised group to operate the ASP.

Class I and III dumps were located a little southeast of Pol-mal. (The U.S. Army supply classification employs ten classes; Class I are items of subsistence; Class III are petroleum products and chemicals.) The task then got under way of trucking forward ammunition, gasoline, and C-rations to stockpile at these forward points.

If the besieged Heartbreak Ridge is envisioned as a medieval fortress, then the central ridgeline made up of Hills 851, 931, and 894 constitute the inner castle keep. The several hills that ring this central ridgeline may be compared to bastions set at intervals in the fortress wall, their guns covering each other to keep at bay an attacking force.

To locate these bastions protecting the central ridgeline, Hill 894 at the ridgeline's southernmost tip may be used as a reference point (see Map 6).

On the Second Division's Left Boundary

Hill 867 a little over 5,000 meters southwest of 894. (This places 867 on Mundung-ni Valley's western side.)

666 just a little north of 867.

1005, 1040 twin peaks 3,200 meters northwest of 867.

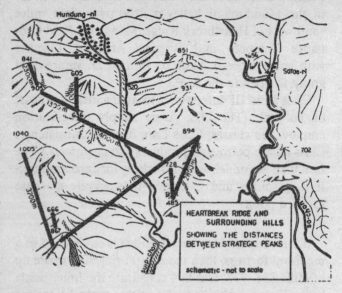

Map 6
The bastions (hills) surrounding Heartbreak Ridge

In the Center Sector

Hill 485   2,800 meters southwest of 894. (Thus, Hill 485 is on the eastern side of Mundung-ni Valley.)

728   1,500 meters due north of 485. (Hill 728's location just 1,800 meters southwest of 894 explains why General Young called it the "key terrain feature in the whole area.")

Crossing over to the western side of Mundung-ni Valley,

Hill 636 4,000 meters northwest from 728.

    905 beyond 636, it is 1,300 meters farther northwesterly.

    841 2,300 additional meters northwesterly. (Thus, 841 is only about 400 meters west of Mundung-ni Village.)

    605 1,800 meters due north from 636.

Major Thomas Mellon's G-3 section worked day and night to formulate the operation plan's details. In the evening of October 2 the Second Division published Operation Order No. 37. The order assigned missions to the three infantry regiments and supporting units as follows (see Map 7):

The Ninth Infantry, under Col. John Lynch, attacking along the division's left boundary was to seize objective A (Hill 867), then objective B (Hills 980, 1005, and 1040).

The Thirty-eighth Infantry, under Col. Frank T. Mildren, pushing up through the center sector, was to seize objective C (Hill 728) and objective F (Hill 485). The directive also ordered the Thirty-eighth to provide infantry support to the Seventy-second Tank Battalion.

The Seventy-second Tank Battalion, commanded by Lt. Col. Joseph W. Jarvis, was ordered to drive up the Mundung-ni Valley and seize objective H (Mundung-ni Village). A platoon of Company D, Second Engineer (Combat) Battalion, became attached to the tank battalion. Companies C and D (-) of Second Engineer (Combat) Battalion were ordered in direct support of the Thirty-eighth Infantry and were to reduce enemy obstacles on the Kongdong–Mundung-ni road.

The Twenty-third Infantry, with enemy pressure upon it finally relieved by the flanking attacks of its sister regiments was at last free to take objective D (Hill 931 and the unnumbered ridgeline running west). Also, the regiment was to seize objective E (the unnumbered ridge south of Hill 851) and to assist the Thirty-eighth Infantry in taking objective C (Hill 728).

Further, the directive assigned normal fire-support roles to the division's artillery battalions: The Fifteenth Field Artillery (FA) Battalion was to fire in direct support of the Ninth Regiment; the Thirty-seventh FA, in direct support of the Twenty-third; and the Thirty-eighth FA, in direct support of the Thirty-eighth Regiment. The 503d FA Battalion was to give general fire support to the entire division.

Reminiscent of Capt. Robert E. Lee and his engineers, whose extraordinary efforts chipped out of the pedregal's stone-hard, volcanic lava an approach to Mexico City in 1847, the Second Division engineers set about preparing the Mundung-ni Valley roadbed. Although the weather in which they worked was not uncomfortable—mostly foggy and damp in the early mornings turning to fair and warm as the day wore on—Lt. Col. Robert Love's combat engineers were under constant observation by the enemy. The North Koreans tried desperately to impede their task by pouring destructive fire into the ranks of laboring men. Still the work went on.

From the very first the engineers exhibited heroism equal to that of their infantry comrades. On October 1, Corp. James Harsh from Ohio was in charge of a Company A, Second Combat Engineers, demolition

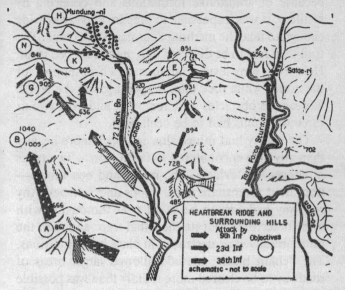

Map 7
Objectives assigned by Operation Touchdown

crew. When they went to blast out rock for a tank route in the lower Mundung-ni Valley, the crew were met by murderous artillery and mortar rounds exploding all around them. Despite the ever-present danger of being injured or killed, Corporal Harsh kept on working in the open, directing his men in the completion of their vital undertaking.[4]

To make the passageway suitable for tank traffic, both natural and artificial obstacles needed to be overcome. Huge boulders were removed either by blasting or with bulldozers, but sometimes hand-wielded picks and shovels were required. At times, because of granitelike formations and cratering by artillery, it was impossible to prepare a roadway wide enough to take the medium Sherman M4A3 tank. The trail then had to be diverted into the stream bed itself. Here rocks were leveled out to make a firm support for the armor while rock piles heaped high by the North Koreans as obstacles were removed, and even two or three waterfalls had to be dealt with.

The enemy had mined this approach more heavily than any area encountered so far in Korea. Two types of concealed devices—Shu-mines and box mines— were used to ensnare U.N. troops and vehicles. Any roadway had first to be swept over thoroughly with mine detectors to locate the lethal traps and then the mines removed or destroyed in place by demolitions. The "chain block" method allowed larger areas of roadway to be cleared more rapidly than was possible by individual mine detection and removal. The engineers placed chain blocks of tetranol at 50-foot intervals on the sides of the trail and then set them off. The explosions detonated the nearby mines.

Other preparations went forward. Private First Class Raymond Myers wrote in his diary the following:

10/2—I saw one of my buddies I came over with, Frank A. He was driving a jeep. I took the major back to Div. Air Port. He got a plane and flew over the front. They laid a six-mile line to Able Co. by airplane and they got it in.

Capt. George B. Daniels, a South Carolinian, one of the pilots from Second Division Air Section, helped lay communications wire from the air. The area in which the infantry units operated was so rugged that to be of any use the wire had to be dropped at rather defined spots so that ground communication crews could retrieve it. Flying his L-plane at dangerously low altitudes and maneuvering around the treacherous mountain peaks, Captain Daniels succeeded in placing the wire where it was needed. The threat of crashing against the mountainside was not the only hazard Daniels faced. As he swept in low, the enemy directed hostile ground fire at his plane.[5]

While Mundung-ni Valley had to await further extensive preparation by the engineers before it could take tank traffic, Satae-ri Valley to the east was already suitable for armor. The Twenty-third Regiment organized Task Force Sturman with the mission of making "softening up" raids ranging all the way to Satae-ri Village in the north. From positions in the northern end of the valley, the tanks could then place fire on the reverse side of the hills constituting Heartbreak Ridge, destroying the enemy's formidable bunkers.

The task force took its name from its commander, Lt. Col. Kenneth R. Sturman, an outgoing leader who inspired confidence in his men. Besides the Twenty-third Tank Company, this infantry-tank team consisted of two platoons from the Second Reconnaissance Company, the French Battalion P and A platoon, and one of the companies of the Ivanhoe Security Force (ISF). The three companies of ISF were made up of all Korean troops except for two Americans assigned to each company. Commanded by 1st

Lt. Arthur C. White, an affable young reserve officer from Jasper, Alabama, who had been a marine in World War II, ISF's mission was to provide security for division headquarters, to form blocking positions, and to patrol beyond the main line of resistance.

At 1545 hours on October 3, two platoons of Sherman tanks, together with one antitank platoon, one ISF platoon, and one platoon of Second Engineers moved up Satae-ri Valley. Coming within range, the Sherman's machine guns and high-velocity 76-mm guns laid down heavy fire onto Hills 656, 785, and 796, knocking out eight enemy bunkers. The next day, Task Force Sturman also moved out. M. Sgt. John Boynton, who was assigned to Second Reconnaissance Company but at this time was on temporary duty with ISF, served as liaison between the tanks and accompanying infantry and maintained radio contact with their base. The tanks moved forward from behind the high ground to enter the valley, while the infantry walked on both flanks and behind the tanks so as to engage any enemy rocket teams lurking in the draws that led off on either side. Sergeant Boynton walked with the troops.

Unexpectedly, small arms fire opened up from the high ground to the right of the valley. It was supposed that this particular area had been neutralized. The sergeant scrambled onto one of the tanks in the column, and as he did so he noticed something very peculiar: Bits of paint from the tank he rode were chipping off. It took a few seconds for him to realize that this was from enemy bullets pinging against the armor. Just then the tanks buttoned up and he leaped to the ground.

The tanks took up positions and began returning fire. The enemy small arms fire increased from the high ground. Having little protection, the infantry ran forward to crouch in a shallow culvert. Meanwhile Boynton reached the field telephone on one tank and tried to alert the tankers that the men would have to pull back, leaving them no infantry protection. But the noise was so great that he was unable to make contact with the tank crew, and so he ran ahead to join the other men in the culvert. A second time he tried to call the tankers by radio, but an enemy bullet tore through the transmitter, rendering it useless.

Another mishap occurred. Thinking the men crouched in the culvert ahead were enemy, a tank began firing into them with its coaxial machine gun. Just in time one of the men tied his bandana to the end of his rifle and started waving it wildly at the closest tank as yet another tank was lowering its cannon and turning it toward the helpless troops. In desperation Sergeant Boynton jumped out of the culvert and started running toward the tanks waving his submachine gun high in the air.

A tank fired. The explosion and accompanying ball of fire blew him over backward, knocking him unconscious. When he came to his senses, Boynton found his steel helmet gone, his eyebrows singed, his ears blistered, and his ears with a constant ringing.

But the tankers had at last realized their mistake. Sergeant Boynton and the others found that their best protection was behind the tanks, though by now they had suffered three wounded and one dead.[6]

In the afternoon of October 4, tanks of Task Force Sturman engaged in a firefight in the Satae-ri Valley with elements of the N.K. *Nineteenth Regiment.* The fight lasted for a full two and one-half hours. In all, the task force's tanks scored direct hits on 14 of the North Korean bunkers.

During one thrust up Satae-ri Valley, Lt. Arthur White rode as bow gunner in 1st Lt. Robert C. Deyo's tank. Lieutenant Deyo was the company executive officer of Second Reconnaissance Company but had been given command of those elements from his company making up a part of Task Force Sturman. When Lieutenant White saw that some of his ISF men were taking heavy casualties from enemy 60-mm mortar fire, he reluctantly left the security of the tank's protecting armor to direct the troops to safer positions.

Sergeant Bererd, an early French Army reserve volunteer for Korea, was riding in a Sherman M4A3, one of ten tanks going up Satae-ri Valley to fire on North Korean positions. As they turned the last bend in the roadway leading to Satae-ri Village, Hill 656—the Watch Dog—came into view. Using their 76-mm guns, the tanks laid down a heavy barrage upon the enemy entrenched on the hill. The tankers' method was to fire two or three shells and then move their vehicle forward to prevent the enemy from zeroing in his own weapons on them.

With their fire mission completed, the two tank

platoons began pulling back. The tank in which Serge Bererd rode stopped prior to taking up a position down the valley. He raised his head up through the hatch and looked around. To the left rear of the tank he saw a tall U.S. sergeant, the assistant platoon leader. Bererd knew him as a personable fellow who was always counting the days he had remaining in Korea before rotating home. The sergeant now had 23 days left to go. To the tank's left front stood two lieutenants talking.

The French sergeant, who spoke English fluently, was about to hoist himself up through the hatch and onto the tank's top when one of the lieutenants distracted him by a jovial remark, "Well, how does an infantryman like going on a cavalry mission?"

Just then a 122-mm mortar round roared overhead and impacted beside the tank. When the dust and debris cleared, Bererd saw a crater, four feet across and nearly a foot deep, in the roadway. One of the lieutenants was lying on the ground wounded, and the other officer was helping him. The tall sergeant with only 23 days left in Korea was sprawled in the roadway, dead.[7]

The infantry battalions used the period from October 1 to October 5 to carry out extensive patrolling, set up ambushes, and resupply themselves with ammunition and rations. The successful ambushes netted many North Korean prisoners who gave valuable information about enemy troop dispositions, strengths, and morale. During the latter half of September the Second U.S. Division and ROK divisions located on its flanks either captured or took the surrender of a total of 671 North Koreans. One day alone, September 19, netted 80 of the enemy who would no longer fight for the communists.

Many of these enemy troops gave themselves up by coming into U.N. lines holding "safe conduct passes" dropped by U.S. aircraft. The communists played this psychological game as well. For the North Koreans scattered thousands of propaganda leaflets at places where they might be picked up by U.N. troops. A message directed to "officers and men of the U.S., British, and other foreign troops on the first anniversary of the Korean War—a war launched by Syngman Rhee at the instigation of Dupont, Rockefeller, Morgan, and Truman clique," proclaimed the following:

Men of good will: You are now on the one-year old Korean battlefront. How many of you first comers are still alive?

The message went on to cite casualty figures and made other propaganda ploys. It ended thus:

The central headquarters of the Korean People's Army will guarantee your safety and will treat you leniently as peace fighters. Your life is only one and not two!

Another leaflet, denoted as a Safe Conduct Pass, exhorted the fighting men to surrender:

Lay down your arms. Live to see your homeland again.

Bud Seybert did expect to see his home again, but only after the defeat of the communists. He sent the message and Safe Conduct Pass home as souvenirs.

Because Operation Touchdown was to be launched at night, Second Division's officers and men needed preparation for night fighting. Third Battalion of the Twenty-third Regiment was especially fortunate, for its commander, Gene Craven, had been an instructor in night operations at the Infantry School, Fort Benning, Georgia, before coming to Korea. After going over the battle plan in detail, Major Craven directed his company officers to spend the rest of the day, a Wednesday, that night, and the next day, which was D minus 1 (the day before the attack), organizing their units and making a dry run in exact battle order on the hills in the area. The object was to thoroughly familiarize everyone with the terrain and let them know who would be to their front, rear, and sides.

Craven went out with a reconnassiance party and selected the battalion's attack position. Officers scanned the hillside to pick out possible bunker locations. They made sketches of their area to take back for briefing their troops. Each platoon and squad leader affirmed to the battalion commander that he thoroughly understood the plan of attack and had instructed his men as to the part each would play.[8]

On October 3rd, U.S. warplanes made preparatory raids on the planned objectives. Thirty-five sorties flew over and hit Hills 728 and 864 and the ridge leading up to 1005. One bomb scored a direct hit in the Fluor Spar mining area, sealing the mine shaft. The Fluor Spar mine, located on the east side of

Mundung-ni Valley about three-fourths of the way up to Mundung-ni Village, had long been used by the communists to store ammunition and supplies and to hide their troops held in reserve.

Colonel Walker reported to General Young that they had been successful in getting a bomber sent over from Japan the preceding night and added, "Corps told us we will get half of the air of the theater." He also reported that his artillery fired 7,100 rounds. October 4 saw 45 airstrikes, which included raids on Hills 728 and 857. The planes hit 851 hard with 500-pound bombs and rockets, and then they strafed it.

The efforts of Lieutenant Colonel Cornelson's logistical personnel proved highly successful. By the evening of October 5 they had trucked in 33,902 rounds of 105-mm and 11,760 rounds of 155-mm ammunition. They stored this prized ammunition at the Ivanhoe Surge Point near Pol-mal, which by now was a fully operational ammunition supply point. In addition, they succeeded in stockpiling at the Class I and Class III supply dumps 20,000 gallons of gasoline and large numbers of C-rations.

As evening's twilight descended upon the stark Korean hills and the mountain peaks' falling shadows lengthened, Second Division waited, all its officers and men satisfied that they were fully prepared for the job ahead. Before dark, F₄U Marine Corsairs zoomed in to napalm, fire rockets at, and machine-gun the enemy positions. Black smoke rose over the hills in the distance and settled down heavily in the valleys.

Second Division's commanding general, anxious

about the successful execution of his well-planned operation, made some final telephone calls in the remaining hours before jump-off: At 1700 hours to General Byers, the X Corps commander, Young declared, "We are all racked up and very confident and ready to go." At 2020 hours to Colonel Adams, the commander of the Twenty-third Regiment, he said, "I know we have made every preparation for this. Have we organized and trained these assault squads to go after those bunkers?" Colonel Adams assured him that they had trained with recoilless rifles, flame throwers, and bazookas.

At 2030 hours in a telephone conversation with the commanding general, Assistant Division Commander Boatner, who was present at the time with the Ninth Infantry Regiment, reported: "Everyone is confident here. I believe that Lynch will have his objective by 1300 tomorrow." At seven minutes before H hour (hour of attack) General Young talked with Colonel Walker, the Divatry commander. Like de Shazo before him, Young valued Walker's advice and counsel and was pleased to hear him say, "I think everything is in good shape and ready to go, General." Young replied, "That is fine. Adams is going to have 931. We will crack this thing." He concluded, "If you have anything to report, don't hesitate, Ted."[9]

The next reports that came in would tell about the success—or failure—of Operation Touchdown. This time everyone counted on success.

8

Operation Touchdown

Touchdown was the culmination of almost 100 days of
continuous combat by the Second Infantry Division.

Virgil E. Craven
Lieutenant Colonel[1]

Exactly at H hour and D day at 2100 hours on October
5, Operation Touchdown got under way as scheduled.
Under cover of darkness, elements of Second Infantry
Division's three regiments moved forward simultaneously toward their assigned objectives.

From Heartbreak Crossroads in Belgium to Heartbreak Ridge in Korea,[2] Frank T. Mildren was in the
midst of it all. In December 1944 the 34-year-old
Lieutenant Colonel Mildren commanded a battalion
in the Thirty-eighth Infantry Regiment, Second Divi-

sion. His men had taken Heartbreak Crossroads. The next day they had to give it back, and in the pullback Mildren was knocked flat on the ground by an exploding shell.[3]

Now, seven years later, on the other side of the globe, Colonel Frank Mildren commanded the Thirty-eighth Infantry Regiment. His regiment was expected to play an important role in taking Heartbreak Ridge. Would history repeat itself?

Even before the official start of the Touchdown operation, Thirty-eighth Regiment had already taken one of its objectives. The day before, on October 4, at 1300 hours, Company F (2/38) commanded by Captain Fuss had dispatched a two-squad patrol to reconnoiter Hill 485. The patrol got a pleasant surprise when it found the little hill unoccupied. Immediately upon receiving information of this welcome discovery, the rest of Company F, along with a heavy machine-gun platoon attached from Company H, moved out. Thus, Thirty-eighth Regiment secured its first objective (Hill 485—objective F) ahead of schedule. General Young reported the news to his superior, General Byers, "Mildren went out and stole 485."[4]

At H hour, First Battalion (1/38) struck out toward Hill 728 (objective C), 1,500 meters to the north of 485. This advance continued throughout the night and early morning, and the battalion encountered little enemy opposition except for some sporadic mortar and long-range small arms fire. By 1000 hours on October 6 they had gotten to within 1,000 yards of Hill 728's top, and at midday lead elements took the objective. Company E (2/38), having been delayed by heavy mortar and small arms fire, succeeded in occupying positions a little southwest of Hill 728 at 1500 hours. But attempts by a patrol from the Second Battalion (2/38) to get up on Hill 636 failed.

Colonel Lynch's Ninth Regiment, employing its First and Third Battalions, likewise moved out on schedule toward their objective, Hill 867 (objective A). Without making contact with the enemy, all companies established perimeter defenses at midnight. Clearly General Young was displeased with Ninth Regiment's failure to keep going. When he talked with Colonel Lynch at 0220 hours, Young expressed surprise that all the Ninth had done was to move to the line of departure and stop. He reiterated that he had visualized all three regiments assaulting their objectives at one time. The commander of the Ninth assured Young that they would move again at daylight, at 0530 hours.

The Ninth Regiment did begin moving again early on the morning of the sixth. Companies A, B, and C (1/9) deployed for the attack on Hill 867. The North Koreans poured down on them a heavy concentration of grenades and small arms and automatic weapons fire. In coordination with the First Battalion, K and I Companies (3/9), which were joined in the afternoon by L, also hit 867. They likewise encountered intense hostile fire.

At 1700 hours Hill 867 still had not been taken. First Battalion had gotten to within 150 yards of the top but remained pinned down by enemy machine guns. At this point General Young was reluctant to let the Thirty-eighth Regiment push out any farther, for he was concerned that until 867 actually fell, Mildren's left flank would be exposed.

There had elapsed 23 days since the time of the initial attack against Hill 931 by Colonel Adams's Twenty-third Regiment in mid-September until its attack against this same hill on D day, October 5. On this occasion the results would prove quite different. Adams made effective use of all four of his battalions. His plan was for the Second and Third Battalions (2/23 and 3/23) to thrust up from the south against Hill 931 while the French Battalion (Fr/23) struck against it from the north. Meanwhile the First Battalion (1/23) would take diversionary action to the north against Hill 851.

The troops had advanced to their attack positions, making use of the evening shadows to help hide their movement from the enemy. Where these dark shadows would fall had been carefully noted during trial runs conducted in the preceding days.

The clear evening meant that radio transmissions would be clear.

Just before the battalions moved out, Hank Daniels, who was commanding the Second Battalion, spoke with Gene Craven, who was commanding the Third Battalion, alluding to Craven's night operations background. "To know that an ol' night owl outfit like yours will go up on that hill gives me the certain feeling we'll be eating breakfast in the gooks' bunkers when the sun comes up."[5] This optimistic prediction would not be far from coming true.

Jumping off at 2111 hours K Company (3/23) advanced westward. Almost immediately the company came under enemy defensive mortar fire. The troops endured the deadly shells falling all around them and continued moving up the slopes. But now the enemy's defense was less effective because its fires had to be scattered against movements across the entire front.

By 2345 K (King) Company had reached the 600-meter level about 1,400 meters southwest of 931's crest. A little later they cut the ridge running west from 931. Here the company established a blocking position to stave off a possible enemy stab from the rear. One North Korean unit in the vicinity was caught by surprise and a fierce fire fight erupted, but King's blocking position effectively cut off the enemy's route of reinforcement to troops on Hill 931. Friendly forces thus controlled all the terrain westward to the Fluor mines and Paeam Village.

L (Love) Company (3/23) followed King onto the ridgeline and turned right toward the objective. With events progressing satisfactorily, Love asked and received permission from Major Craven to push on to the peak of 931. Colonel Daniels had received the signal at 0310 hours to move his Second Battalion. Within 30 minutes Company G flame throwers (2/23) were in action. F Company passed through G to press the attack, and the North Koreans reacted with a heavy volume of small arms and automatic weapons fire.

As this hail of bullets continued to spew from the defending bunkers, one private in Company F realized that the only way to stop it was to knock out the emplacements protecting the firers. He took it upon himself to take action. And so gathering up an armful of hand grenades, Private First Class Gerald Underwood from Missouri crawled out in front of his own positions. With bullets whizzing across his body, he inched his way to within a few yards of an enemy bunker and threw first one, and then several other, well-placed grenades into the enemy bunker's firing aperture.

Underwood saw North Koreans run out of the bunker under attack, trying to reach the safety of another one of their emplacements. Heady now with the success of his own performance, the private stood up, fully exposing himself. Taking his carbine from off his back, Underwood fired volley after volley at the fleeing enemy, killing and wounding some of them.[6] Heroic actions such as this helped F Company move on to and secure the northern slope of 931 with the aid of the French Battalion's Second Company, which came down from the north taking some prisoners in the process.

Daylight of October 6 found the three battalions, Second (2/23), Third (3/23), and French (FR/23), fully entrenched on 931's crest, its south and north knobs, and the east-west ridgeline running to the Fluor Spar mine. All of objective D—the central and highest peak of Heartbreak Ridge—was at last in U.N. hands.

Helicopters swooped in and took out Third Battalion's wounded. Gene Craven displaced his command post to the top of 931, setting it up in the North Korean commander's former bunker. When Hank Daniels joined him later that morning, they ate some rations and jokingly called it "breakfast."[7]

General Young did not restrain his praise for the Twenty-third Regiment. The next day he told Colonel Adams, "I think your people put on one of the finest night attacks. That was a fine operation. Yours was the only one that was successful. You saved a lot of people doing that, Jim."[8]

The Ninth Regiment was a different story. Throughout the day of October 6, the fact that Colonel Lynch had not yet taken objective A (Hill 867) continued to plague General Young. He talked to Ninth Infantry's commander or its operations officer (S–3) at least six times that day, and in the evening he called General Boatner, who had continued to remain at Ninth Regiment's headquarters. (Ed Rowney, the executive officer of the Thirty-eighth, denoted Boatner's role as that of a troubleshooter.[9])

Young complained to his assistant commander that "867 is holding everything up. That is the only thing keeping Mildren from going full scale."

However, Task Force Sturman's day ended quite successfully. The tank-infantry team had departed at first light on another one of its now-famous raids into Satae-ri Valley. Within two hours, at 0825, the North Koreans poured a barrage of 122-mm mortars onto the tanks, disabling three of them. The task force pushed right on through this barrage to take up firing positions. Its tank-mounted 76-mm guns then blasted away at the enemy's bunkers on Hills 656, 841, and 811, knocking out 35 bunkers and 5 known machine-gun positions. Before withdrawing for the night, the task force recovered its three disabled tanks.

The North Koreans sought to get rid of this menace,

Task Force Sturman, by trying to slip 80 of their men into the Satae-ri Valley to knock out the tanks while they sat in their night positions. The French pioneer platoon was ready for this very thing. The Frenchmen caught the infiltrators in an ambush, completely halting them. Of the French pioneer platoon, Colonel Adams said, "They are a remarkable bunch."[10]

Sunday, October 7 came. But this was no day of rest for the weary officers and men of the U.S. Second Infantry Division and its attached French Battalion. The Second Division's commander interrupted his early morning meeting with his staff officers to take a call from the ADC, General Boatner. When Young hung up, he announced, "They got 867!" Then pointing his finger to a symbol on the briefing map depicting Ninth Infantry's First Battalion, he stated confidently, "This battalion, in conjunction with the Second Battalion of the Ninth, will push on to 1005. That frees the Thirty-eighth Infantry from a flank threat."

This staff briefing disclosed some additional highly interesting information. Lieutenant Colonel Aykrod, G–2, reported that the Military police (MPs) had on the day before apprehended behind friendly lines three North Koreans. These were, he revealed, bonafide N.K. agents dressed in U.S. clothing, carrying military payment certificates and having U.S. weapons and equipment. Also, an MP jeep had been ambushed in the Pia-ri Valley. One MP was missing and one dead. Colonel Aykrod warned, "Maintain double vigilance in CP and bivouac areas."[11]

Second Division published additional instructions

relating to Operation Touchdown that gave the Thirty-eighth Regiment three new objectives: objective G, which was Hills 905 and 974 and the long, curving ridgeline between these two hills; objective K, which was Hill 605; and objective N, which was Hill 841 (see Map 7).

The Seventy-second Tank Battalion became attached to the Thirty-eighth Regiment at 0600 hours on October 7. The regiment and its attached battalion were directed to prepare plans for a joint attack on Mundung-ni Village (objective H).

With 867 in friendly hands, the division's three infantry regiments were now poised to continue on to their next objectives: the Ninth Regiment to Hills 1005 and 1040; the Thirty-eighth Regiment to the several hills on the western side of Mundung-ni Valley; and the Twenty-third Regiment to Hill 851, the final peak at the north end of the Heartbreak ridgeline.

With altitude only a little less than 931, Hill 851 was just as steep and its sharp granite sides just as difficult to climb. Two very prominent boulders dominated 851's crest, giving this distinctive landmark its nickname, The Teeth.

On Second Division's far left boundary, Ninth Infantry's Second Battalion (2/9) made a sweeping movement through the Eighth ROK Division sector and approached the ridgeline between 867 and 1005 from the west. Corporal James Rhea, an Oklahoma Sooner, was in a demolition squad in Headquarters Company, Second Battalion. At this time Corporal

Rhea and his squad were attached to Company F. As enemy mortar rounds started coming in upon them, several men in Company F received serious injuries. Rhea seemed not to notice the mortar shells exploding around him, though, as he administered first aid to his injured comrades. He improvised litters and directed the removal of the casualties back to the battalion aid station.[12]

Second Battalion of the Ninth (2/9) succeeded in cutting the ridgeline between Hills 867 and 1005. They then prepared to move northwesterly toward 1005.

Meanwhile, in Second Division's center sector, Mildren's Thirty-eighth Regiment prepared for its forward movement. Second Battalion (2/38) assaulted Hill 636 to the northwest across the shallow Suipchon River. Defensive automatic weapons, small arms, and mortars forced the attackers to withdraw by 1500 hours.

Leaving one platoon of Company C, supported by some heavy weapons of Company D on Hill 728, Companies A, B, and C (-) (1/38) shifted to take up reserve positions. Even when not in contact with the enemy, infantry are likely to take casualties. And so it happened that descending a hill from their old positions, Company A stumbled into a minefield. A single ear-splitting explosion, and the men saw the lieutenant who was leading the column knocked hard to the ground. He was obviously badly hurt. Without orders Pvt. Floyd Beach took it upon himself to enter the minefield to go to the aid of the lieutenant. As he approached the wounded officer, a second loud explosion split the air. Private Beach had set off another mine. His injuries killed him.[13]

At noon this Sabbath day, Brig. Gen. Haydon Boatner, the ADC, came up to the crest of Hill 931 to the North Korean commander's bunker, taken over by Major Craven as his battalion command post. In his usual blustery manner Boatner said to Craven, "This is the first damn time I have been an aide to a lieutenant colonel." Then he took out of his pocket a pair of silver leaves. "General Young dispatched me to pin these on you, Gene."[14]

Boatner pinned the leaves on Craven, and the Third Battalion commander became a lieutenant colonel. It was the second time in his military career that Eugene Craven received a battlefield promotion. On a European battlefield in World War II, General Patton had given him a captain's railroad tracks.

Afterward they proudly showed off the captured North Korean bunkers to the ADC. Only from a close-up inspection did the U.S. troops fully realize just how sturdily these bunkers were built. After Hill 931 had been taken, during the enemy's counterattack some U.S. officers were inside one captured bunker. Three enemy 121-mm mortar shells had hit the emplacement directly. One of the officers reported later, "It didn't even shake."

The Twenty-third Regiment allowed itself no let-up after securing Hill 931. Immediately the encirclement of 851 began as a first step in bringing about that fortress's downfall. With a platoon of L Company in the lead, Third Battalion (3/23) moved out with the object of cutting the ridgeline at the 700-meter level running west from 851. The enemy resisted this advance with intense fire from automatic weapons and mortars.

I Company attempted to move up to the left (west) of L, but was driven back in its first try. Third Battalion's remaining rifle company, King, then passed through the positions of L Company, which had consolidated its gains on the ridgeline. King attacked to the east toward Hill 851 but was halted by enemy artillery and mortar fire. Task Force Sturman, having moved up the Satae-ri Valley at 0930, now placed tank fire on 656 and the other hills making up the high ground to the north and east. This action was very effective in diverting the enemy's fire from the attacking companies on the ridgeline.

Third Battalion continued to press hard its attack during the night and morning of October 7–8. After five attempts I Company finally succeeded at 0415 hours in getting on the ridgeline to the left of Love—L Company—taking up a position about halfway between Hill 851 and the Fluor Spar mine.

Meanwhile, First Battalion (1/23) was attacking 851 directly from the south. From out of the strongly fortified enemy bunkers poured a shower of hand grenades as well as a hail of automatic weapons bullets. C Company repeatedly assaulted these bunkers, which guarded a small ridge just south of the main 851 peak. Each time the infantrymen got to within 75 yards of the bunkers, the North Koreans left their fortifications to engage the attackers in hand-to-hand combat, driving them back. Finally C Company succeeded in digging in about 50 yards from this bunker line. They were now 400 yards from the peak of Hill 851.

For the past several days there had been repeated reports of sightings and information from prisoners of war indicating that Chinese communist forces (CCF) were coming into this sector of the U.N. front. This morning, October 8, the intelligence report noted that the CCF were apparently reconnoitering the battle positions of the North Koreans. This suggested to G–2 that "the CCF plan to move through the N.K.s [North Koreans] and launch an attack." The report concluded, "The probability is that they will relieve the N.K.s in place. N.K. *V Corps* is in bad shape. Their casualties yesterday were 275 KIA, 500 WIA and 18 POWs captured. The enemy continues attempts to infiltrate our rear areas."[15]

From left to right across the divisions front the three infantry regiments continued their contact with the enemy. Meeting only light resistance, Ninth Infantry's B Company (1/9) seized Hill 666, standing just a little north of 867.

The story of Second Battalion's (2/9) assault on Hill 1005 was quite different. Companies F and G met stiff enemy resistance consisting of small arms, automatic weapons, and mortar fire. Private First Class Herbert Willis, point man in one of G Company's squads, kept on pushing forward despite the murderous fire. A mortar shell exploded nearby, injuring him, but Willis refused offers to be evacuated. Instead he kept on shooting at the enemy, killing and wounding several of them.[16]

Another G Company man, Pvt. Raymond Cotta, refused treatment of his wounds, and instead carried another, more seriously injured comrade out of an exposed area as mortar shells exploded around him.[17] When enemy bullets struck down a radioman, Company G's communications chief, Corp. Curtis Burtness crawled out into the small clearing where the wounded man lay. Working amidst a hail of steel from the enemy machine guns, Curtis gave the radioman first aid and then moved him back to safety. After that the corporal carried many important messages for his unit and continued doing so despite himself being knocked from a ridge by a bursting mortar shell.[18]

Later George—G Company—became completely pinned down. Fox, moving through George to continue the assault, likewise met heavy enemy defensive fires. A bursting shell sent fragments of hot steel into Corp. Paul Daughty's body. Although in pain Daughty rushed forward and directed a hand grenade into the North Korean bunker firing on his company. The well-placed grenade silenced this one enemy firepoint.

Like George, its sister company, Fox also became pinned down. Next, E Company attempted to pass through F. Darkness closed in and all three of Second Battalion's rifle companies dug in.

When morning came, Lt. Col. Rowney, the executive officer of the Thirty-eighth Infantry, reported that the Second Battalion (2/38) was "right up against 636 on the knob to the north."[19] Lieutenant Morgan's Company K and Lieutenant Clark's Company L of the Third Battalion (3/38) had reached Hill 605 (objective K).

Some communication problems developed between regimental headquarters and its battalions, so that Thirty-eighth Regiment's commanding officer, Colonel Mildren, went up to Second Battalion to be at the forefront of the action. Maj. Warren Hodges, who was tall and large, weighing over 200 pounds, commanded that battalion. Ed Rowney thought him to be "an amusing sort, warm hearted, popular with his troops." A practical joker, Hodges was a favorite with Frank Mildren.[20]

But personal friendship did not prevent Mildren from insisting that Hodges make inspections of his troops on foot even though the heavy battalion commander had trouble with his feet, which even bled with much use. As consolation Mildren would walk with the major, who then had the problem of keeping up with the agile colonel.

Completion of the engineer work on the Mundung-ni trail so that Seventy-second Tank Battalion could strike up that valley concerned everyone. Lieutenant Colonel Rowney reported to division that with 200 yards left to go, the engineers needed 2,000 pounds more explosives. Division in turn asked X Corps for assistance in getting shape charges.

The day ended with Second Battalion (2/38) sitting on Hill 636. It planned to strike out to the northwest for 905 the next morning. The Thirty-eighth alerted its attached Netherlands detachment to move at 0400 hours and assume a position between Second Battalion (2/38) on 636 and Third Battalion (3/38) at Hill 605. In this way the Dutch detachment could protect Second Battalion's right flank and assist in its attack on 905.

The Twenty-third Regiment's Third Battalion (3/23) spent the day, October 8, resupplying with rations and ammunition. In a conversation with General Young, Colonel Adams said he wanted to build up supplies before the final assault on 851. General Young agreed completely, adding, "Let's play it cagey."

The Second Division commander then cautioned Adams to "button up good." When he asked if Twenty-third had patrols out front, Adams explained graphically their situation: "There would be no use in that, sir. We are eyeball to eyeball with the enemy, and each of us knows where the other is."

Then at 1945 hours while Love and King Companies were adjusting their positions, the North Koreans struck. A mass of screaming enemy soldiers came at them from the northeast. The counterattack lasted 30 minutes before being successfully repulsed.

Another company-size counterattack struck Love at 2300 hours but was repulsed in 15 minutes. The upshot of this night's action was that instead of losing ground, friendly forces gained 100 yards and G Company (2/23), which had become attached to Third Battalion, closed in behind King.

At midnight the eerie wail of bugles, like howling

coyotes, sounded in the dark. No further attacks came that night.

The G–2 report at General Young's staff briefing on October 9 gave a follow-up report on possible Communist Chinese intervention. A captured Chinese POW revealed that the *Third Battalion, 610th Regiment, 204th Division* of the *68th* CCF army was due to arrive in that sector of the battlefield on October 12. General Boatner observed, "Experience has shown us that the CCF aren't as tough as the N.K.s."

General Young's remarks were stronger: "I'd welcome any change from N.K. to CCF. They should be easier to shoot up. We'll put them all in the same damned meat grinder as we did the rest of them."[21]

Later, in recounting the North Korean's strong counterattack of the night before, Colonel Adams said, "I'm inclined to think they were pushed forward by the Chinese."

As in the preceding days, fighter bombers flew close support missions onto the Ninth Regiment's objectives. Using machine guns, rockets, 500-pound bombs, and napalms they succeeded in softening up enemy emplacements on Hills 1005 and 1040. Moving abreast, companies E, F, and G (2/9) got on the bottom part of 1005 at about 0900 hours on the morning of the ninth.

To assist Second Battalion, First Battalion (1/9) swung around to go for 1040, situated just a little way to the northwest and being a part of the same hill mass as 1005. Against a virtual wall of fire, 2/9 climbed up Hill 1005's side (objective B). In a determined bayonet assault, the battalion seized this objective in the afternoon.

Colonel Mildren moved out his Thirty-eighth Regiment early on the morning of the ninth. At 0400 the Second Battalion (2/38) attempted to cut the ridgeline running from 905 to 605 by advancing against enemy mortar, artillery, and machine-gun fire. At 1700 hours Company F became engaged in hand-to-hand fighting, using hand grenades and small arms fire. But then at 1820 hours the North Koreans struck Fox from three different directions and the company was ordered to pull back and go in perimeter defense.

On that day the Twenty-third Regiment's Third Battalion occupied itself mainly in consolidating its positions on the ridgeline west of 851. At 1800 hours I Company jumped off to secure two knobs just north of the Fluor Spar mine area. This action was delayed by flame-thrower malfunction until more flame throwers could be brought up for use.

Once again Task Force Sturman thrust up the Satae-ri Valley so that its tanks could fire on Hill 851 as well as the other hills surrounding the valley. This day the task forces' fires, in coordination with fires from the First Battalion (1/23), knocked out 8 bunkers on 851. Whereas on the preceding day these same fire sources had destroyed 18 enemy bunkers. But many bunkers still remained intact on Hill 851. Before Twenty-third Regiment could secure the hill, every one of these emplacements would have to be reduced.

Getting supplies at the proper time and place is always a matter of concern in combat. Often the intricacies of a problem are seen quite differently at higher echelons than at lower-unit levels. X Corps headquarters kept urging air drops from C-119s as the solution to the battalions' constant needs for resupply. The Korean laborers—the choggy bearers —were often unreliable because they might run at the first sign of enemy fire.

Division command, in response to the Corps's suggestion, would, in turn, try to get the regiments to make arrangements for C-119 drops. Seemingly to encounter resistance, General Young put the question directly to Colonel Mildren: "Your supply people said all they wanted is an L-plane. Why not a C-119?"

Mildren's frank response was, "We have found that gathering the stuff up takes just as long as it would to carry it in the first place."[22]

Second Engineer's construction of the Mundung-ni Valley roadway was nearing completion. The demolition charges that had been urgently requested from X Corps were found in the engineers' own rear area. And now only one narrow defile at the upper end of the valley remained to be cleared.

When the engineers entered the defile, a heavy concentration of enemy artillery and mortar fire began to fall upon them. A lieutenant platoon leader and his assistant were wounded. Corp. Robert Bartley, a medic, went immediately to aid the wounded men. He got together a litter team that quickly moved the injured men out of the danger area. Although the lieutenant died, the quick action of Corp. Bartley saved the life of the other man.[23]

Raymond Myers, the ninth-grade dropout, in his

matter-of-fact manner of reporting, sometimes mixed
the bizarre with the commonplace:

10/9—Drove the jeep all day. We had chicken for
supper. Draper got killed. A round hit right in his
hole. All I could find was one little piece of meat.
Nothing else.

9

~~~~~~~~

An End Run

The doughboy likes the tank to move forward with him,
and his trusty rifle is a guarantee against attempts by the
enemy antitank squads to knock out that tank.

Sam Freedman, Captain,
Seventy-second Tank Battalion[1]

When the early morning's gray fog lifted, allowing the
men on Heartbreak Ridge to see into the valley below,
a spectacular sight greeted their eyes, a most welcome
sight.

They saw sitting there on the Mundung-ni Valley
trail a long column of Sherman M4A3 tanks, their big
V–8 engines warming up as tank commanders and
crew waited in anticipation. The day before, the

Second Combat Engineer Battalion commander, Lt. Col. Robert Love, had given the green light. The trail now lay open for a distance of six miles—all the way from Imokchong in the south to Mundung-ni in the north. The engineers' unprecedented achievement had made the roadbed ready for armor traffic.

At 0600 hours on October 10, the medium tanks of Lt. Col. Joseph Jarvis's Seventy-second Tank Battalion rumbled forward. They moved ever so cautiously at first, but as tank drivers became convinced that the path was indeed clear of mines and obstacles, they shifted to speedier gear. B Troop provided the armor thrust accompanied by L Company, Thirty-eighth Regiment, for infantry support against enemy anti-tank teams, and a platoon from D Company, Second Engineers, to assist in clearing any previously unidentified obstacles along the way.

The column reached the Fluor Spar mine area. Turret guns turned and gunners blasted away at the abandoned mine from which the mineral fluorite had once been dug. The mine burst into flames. No longer would it provide shelter for North Korean replacement troops or be used for storage of supplies.

Lieutenant Colonel Rowney, executive officer (ExO), Thirty-eighth Regiment, relayed to General Young, the Second Division Commander, the information, "We have two platoons firing and moving north at about 41st grid."

General Young instructed, "We don't want those tanks to come back any further than is necessary for them to get infantry protection. If they need gas, maintenance or ammunition, all that should be taken forward to them."[2]

As the armor column cleared the defile in front of Mundung-ni, it came under enemy long-range artillery and heavy mortar fire. One of the lead tanks was moving forward, firing rapidly, with its hatch open. A single mortar shell dropped right into the hatch opening. The explosion within the confined space killed three tankers and wounded the fourth.

Nonetheless B troop rolled on. Despite increasing hostile artillery and mortars, thickened by small arms and automatic weapons fire, its tank gunners succeeded in lobbing hundreds of high explosive shells onto known areas of enemy troop concentration. Friendly fire was guided by a radio relay station in an observation post (OP) placed well forward on some high ground overlooking the valley and manned by two Seventy-second Battalion staff officers. From this OP the two officers could scan the Mundung-ni Valley floor, spot the enemy troops, and ensure accurate placement of fire.

When the Seventy-second's armor rolled through the village of Mundung-ni, terror-stricken communists were seen fleeing in panic. It was later learned that the surprise appearance of tanks to their rear had caught in the open the Chinese troops of the CCF *204th Division*, 68th Army, who were then in the process of replacing the rapidly disintegrating elements of the N.K. *V Corps*.

By 1300 hours one platoon of B had advanced north of Mundung-ni and found itself in difficult, unprepared terrain. Continuing to receive heavy fire from the enemy as its own ammunition became exhausted, all tanks pulled back to go into night positions, protected by the infantry.

Major Craven, who witnessed the armor thrust, observing it from the vantage point of his battalion command post atop 931, said, "If one single thing convinced my battalion that we would go all the way—right to the top of 851—it was the sight of those tanks operating where the Reds had been certain no tanks could come.

"What a sight those tanks were!"[3]

Capt. Sam Freedman, who served in the Seventy-second Tank Battalion at Heartbreak Ridge, summed up the effect achieved by infantry tank operations like this one:

> Infantry moves forward to the attack with spirit and confidence and a more marked willingness to 'give 'em hell' when tanks are moving with them. If enemy tanks appear they do not have the effect of slowing an advance. Friendly tanks take them on, and the advance can go on to the swift conclusion desired. Enemy emplacements, pillboxes and bunkers are quickly neutralized by powerful tank guns, when troops in such instances might otherwise be pinned down.[4]

Colonel Mildren gave the Second Division commander the results of that day's tank operation in Mundung-ni Valley. He reported that they had a total of 30 tanks operating, and of these, 5 had been put out of commission, including 2 that were hit by antitank weapons and therefore had to be destroyed completely.

General Young responded, "You tell Jarvis I said 'congratulations.'"[5]

Congratulations also went that day to Col. John Lynch, the commander of the Ninth Infantry Regiment. In the morning Companies B and C of the First Battalion (1/9) moved out against Hill 1040. Almost immediately they came under small arms fire from the entrenched enemy. Despite this fire the two companies advanced steadily toward their goal. By 1400 hours lead elements of Company B gained the top of the hill and were followed a short time later by the remainder of the company, as well as by Company C.

The Ninth Regiment spent the rest of the day in mopping-up operations, so that by the time they went into defensive night positions their objective was securely in hand.

With the taking of Hills 1005 and 1040 (objective B) the Ninth Infantry Regiment had secured its final objective in Operation Touchdown. General Young discussed with Colonel Lynch his plan to pull the entire Ninth off the line and give its sector to the Thirty-eighth Regiment.

On the morning of October 10, the Third Battalion of the Thirty-eighth (3/38) resumed its attack on Hill 605. Item Company jumped off at 0630 hours and met a murderous hail of small arms, automatic weapons, and mortar fire; grenades were also being hurled at them. When his squad became pinned down, Corp. Patrick Vaughan stood up in the midst of all the flying steel. Blasting away with a previously captured machine gun as he moved toward the enemy, he killed or wounded many of them. Encouraged by Corp. Vaughan's actions, his squad overran the enemy positions.[6]

After an all-day fight King Company secured Hill 605 (objective K) at 2200 hours. Item cleaned up the hill's fingers that ran north and northeast. In these positions, Third Battalion (3/38-L) was able to tie in with the Dutch detachment on its left and with its own L Company, attached to the Seventy-second Tank Battalion, on its right.

Meanwhile the Second Battalion (2/38) was moving forward against Hill 905. When the loader and gunner of one 57-mm recoilless rifle squad in Company F were wounded, the squad's ammunition bearer, Pfc. William Sullivan, took over operation of the weapon. Although he knew that the recoilless rifle was not an assault weapon and that its back blast would attract the enemy's attention, bringing their fire upon him, he carried it up the hill, stopping to fire into enemy emplacements. Setting the rifle upon an exposed knoll, he continued to fire at the North Korean troops. Time and time again Pfc. Sullivan went back down the hill to obtain ammunition for other firers as well as for himself. On one of his trips down the hill he came upon a wounded soldier and carried him to where the man could receive medical aid.[7]

Both E and F Companies were hit by a strong enemy counterattack. The company commander of each of these companies was lost from wounds received in action. And in each company it was necessary to replace the company commander with a less experienced man. According to Colonel Mildren, "That is what caused the Second Battalion to catch hell."

The companies had to withdraw to defensive positions. By 1700 hours they had consolidated their positions but under heavy mortar and machine gun fire were forced to withdraw even farther, taking up blocking positions some 800 meters south and east of the objective.

The Twenty-third Regiment remained closed-in tight around the Teeth (crest) of Hill 851. As Colonel Adams put it, they were eyeball to eyeball with the enemy. Elements of the regiment occupied most of a spur or finger that slanted down to the west from 851 terminating in a flat knob, designated Hill 520. Here, the North Koreans still held a firm grip.

Company G drew the assignment of taking Hill 520.[8] Two other Second Battalion (2/23) companies were to support the attack: Company E by providing fire from a parallel ridge 500 yards to the south, and Company F by taking up positions just behind G, prepared to pass through and continue the assault.

In the absence of G's company commander, who had gone to Japan on R&R (rest and recuperation) Lt. Raymond W. Riddle, its ExO, became the company's acting commander. There lay 200 yards between G's LD (line of departure) and the flat-topped Hill 520. After a ten-minute preparation by fires from the artillery, heavy machine guns, and Company E's 57-mm recoilless rifles, Corp. David Lamb, acting platoon leader, double-timed Third Platoon forward to a small knoll about halfway between the LD and the objective.

Upon reaching the intermediate knoll, Third Platoon set up a machine gun and fired on Hill 520. (To enable friendly supporting fire elements to identify the forward position of the attacking platoon, one of its men, Private First Class Harry Schmidt, wore a yellow panel around his waist). Corporal Lamb then sent one squad around the left side of the objective while the rest of Third Platoon fired on bunkers at the hill's east end. The enemy reacted with a brisk return fire that wounded several men in the attacking squad as well as some of the men back on the intermediate knob. Lamb radioed Lieutenant Riddle for reinforcements.

At this point, First Platoon moved out. The platoon leader, Lieutenant Jay M. Gano, was so new that a private, Cliff R. High, who had been running the platoon in the absence of an officer, continued to do so. Not far from the LD two men were seriously wounded, and before the platoon reached the intermediate knob, Lieutenant Gano was killed in this, the first minutes of his first combat action. The platoon stopped moving, pinned down by enemy fire.

Smoke from a brush fire drifted north and obscured the pinned-down platoon. Lieutenant Riddle took a chance in ordering his machine guns to fire, placing an accurate fusillade, as it turned out, on Hill 520. Under cover of the machine-gun fire and the smoke's haze High worked Third Platoon forward. Enemy mortar shells started falling upon them, wounding six men. With only 11 men left besides himself, High joined Lamb and his 12 men on the knoll.

Deploying their men in a skirmish line, firing their weapons as they moved forward, High and Lamb directed the assault on the objective. Halfway across the 60 yards of open ground to the hill's forward slope the enemy's automatic weapons opened fire, but they did not stop the advance. Then the North Koreans threw fragmentation and concussion grenades as the skirmish line reached the base of the knoll. One grenade wounded Corp. Lamb, while another grenade broke both Corp. Arne Severson's legs as he walked forward, all the time firing his machine gun.

When this assault faltered, Pvt. High made a second attempt using about a dozen of his men in an enveloping movement that was hidden from the defender's view. As they climbed the hill and moved north to 520, a concussion grenade knocked down Pvt. High. He regained consciousness and again led the platoon. With the help of several flame-thrower operators who had joined them, they destroyed some of the enemy bunkers. When the flame-throwers malfunctioned, a BAR team knocked out one bunker while Pvt. Joe Gaolina silenced another bunker with a well-placed hand grenade.

Pvt. High, with only four or five men, made the final assault on 520 as a few other men fired their rifles and BARs in support. The attackers found eight North Koreans still with their weapons in their hands huddled in front of the bunker that had been the enemy's command post. The North Koreans surrendered. Other enemy troops fled over the hill toward the northwest. At 1600 hours Company G had secured Hill 520.

At this exact time, also, First Battalion (1/23) began an assault on Hill 851. A little later the alert went out to the French Battalion to attack on the east flank of First Battalion. The French commandant, Oliver Le Mire, accompanied the battalions to observe this action.

Side by side, shoulder to shoulder, climbed Frenchman and American, officer and enlisted man. The U.S. troops who were constantly swearing about everything—"cursing with each step"—especially one tall blond sergeant named Gilbert, intrigued Le Mire. As the French officer walked beside Gilbert, he asked the U.S. sergeant why he complained so much.

Gilbert answered, "Because, after all, we've got to go, and the sooner we take this damned ridge, the sooner it will all be finished."

As the two stumbled on up the hill over pieces of shattered rock and broken tree limbs, the sergeant continued, "Of course, sir, work is work. I know that. But it gives me a bellyache to climb up this rotten mountain. It makes me feel better when I complain."

The next day, interspersed with his recordings of tactics and unit movements to go into the annals of military history, Le Mire took time to note (sadly, it seems) the casualty of one particular U.S. soldier. "Gilbert, the big blond American, who was complaining so much yesterday, is killed while moving forward with his machine gun." With amusement Le Mire recalled that the U.S. sergeant had referred to his activity as "working."[9]

The attack by First Battalion (1/23) was stopped before it hardly got started. It could not get over the three little humps that barred access to the ridge toward the rocky teeth. The planned attack by the French Battalion was therefore called off.

Task Force Sturman and the French Pioneer Section moving up Satae-ri Valley received a counterattack at about 1300 hours from 200 enemy. They were subjected two hours later to an intense artillery bombardment in which one tank exploded and the French Pioneer Section became reduced to 14 men. When Commandant Beaufond asked to have them relieved, the Twenty-third Regiment tankers objected, "Let us keep them. These fourteen men are good enough for us."[10]

Second Division directed its chief effort on October 11 to taking Hill 905, which Major Mellon, G-3, called a "big nut to crack." At 0630 hours two patrols from the Thirty-eighth Regiment's Company E and one from Company F reconnoitered the area to the front. Second Battalion (2/38) then moved forward against 905, encountering heavy resistance.

With the Netherlands detachment and Thirty-eighth Tank Company supporting the attack with fire, Second Battalion succeeded in taking 905. Then First Battalion (1/38), which had been in regimental reserves for the preceding five days, passed through Second Battalion to continue the attack 1,000 to

1,200 meters to the north against the high ground (900-meter level) between Hills 905 and 974.

The enemy continued to put up a stiff resistance. As Sgt. Edward B. Rakowiecki climbed up the ridge's slope with his machine-gun squad from Company B, 38th Infantry, the squad suffered many casualties and enemy fire destroyed their machine gun. Sgt. Rakowiecki picked up an abandoned automatic rifle and kept going up the hill despite the enemy bullets whizzing past him. He bravely charged several enemy bunkers, neutralizing them so that his company could continue its advance. Miraculously, Sgt. Rakowiecki received no injuries despite his exposure all this time to the enemy's close fire.[11]

Another B Company man, Charles E. McAuliff, a twenty-three year old draftee from Red Wood City, California, continuously fired his 57-mm recoilless rifle without receiving any injury throughout this attack and later attacks made by the Thirty-eighth Regiment in Operation Touchdown.

First Battalion secured the ridgeline at 1700 hours. The Thirty-eighth Regiment now held all of its objective G. Company B dug in and remained on the ridge overnight while Companies A and C took up blocking positions in the vicinity of Hill 905.

General Young made the decision that with the capture of Hill 905 he would halt the Thirty-eighth Regiment on a line running through Hills 605 and 905. The entire Ninth Regiment would then be pulled back to undergo extensive training. The move off the line of Ninth Regiment had already begun with elements of the Eighth ROK Division relieving First Battalion (1/9) in their positions on Hill 1005. The X Corps commander, General Byers, approved the plan.

On their second day's foray up the western valley, the Seventy-second's tanks drove even farther, north and west, beyond Mundung-ni. The element of surprise initially enjoyed by the armored patrols soon vanished, for the enemy reacted to the onslaught by laying additional mines and employing tank killer teams. The recklessness demonstrated by these antitank infantry teams indicated that they were green and had been poorly trained. This was clear evidence that enemy losses had been heavy and that the North Koreans were having difficulty providing adequate replacements.

L Company (3/38), accompanying the Seventy-second Battalion, received an order to burn all civilian houses in the vicinity. The dry thatched roofs of 35 huts, from which the Korean civilians had previously been evacuated, were readily set ablaze. It was suspected that the North Koreans were using the houses to store supplies and ammunition. Secondary explosions erupting from out of the burning huts proved that this suspicion had been correct.

October 11 marked the beginning of the end for the long ordeal on Hill 851. Preliminary to the attack, Maj. George H. Williams, Jr., the commander of the First Battalion (1/23), had called for an artillery preparation. In addition, the battalion had directed fire from Task Force Sturman's tanks onto the enemy emplacements. These tanks destroyed seven enemy bunkers by direct fire from their 76-mm guns.

At 1610 hours First Battalion launched its attack. B and C Companies moving abreast, went forward 100 meters to the little hillocks lying in front of Hill 851's crest. Two hours later Company C became pinned down, but Company A rushed forward and passed through C to continue the attack with B. Able and Baker—A and B Companies—gained the south slope of 851 but were driven back by intense automatic weapons and small arms fire coming from the enemy bunkers.

At 1700 hours the French Battalion was alerted to assist in the attack.

Of all the battlefields on which he had fought, Commandant Maurice L. Barthélémy, the deputy commander of the French Battalion, disliked Heartbreak Ridge most of all. Having keen gray eyes, a small but strong chin, and an aquiline nose with a high nasal bridge, Barthélémy's appearance was what most Americans would expect of an aristocratic French Army officer. Barthélémy had suffered a serious left shoulder wound while fighting the German invaders of his homeland in May and June of 1940. Later he joined the French Resistance to continue the struggle for freedom. The determined French officer's injuries rendered his left arm almost useless. Walking ramrod, carrying his left shoulder a little higher than the right, Commandant Barthélémy wore his combat wounds like a badge of honor. He considered it a commander's duty, and something of a pleasure, to mix with all his troops every day when they were in contact with the enemy. Heartbreak Ridge made this impossible because its terrain corridors separated the various troop sections, not allowing free movement from one group of men to the other.

The Heavy Weapons Company (C.A.) of the French Battalion had established a fire base, located southeast of Hill 851, consisting of two 75-mm recoilless rifles, two .50-caliber machine guns, and four .30-caliber machine guns. Its 81-mm mortars were positioned a little farther to the rear. All fires had been registered prior to dark, so that when called for they were able to lay down a barrage with remarkable precision. The mortar fires were placed for maximum effect only a few tens of meters in front of the advancing infantrymen.

Led by the First Company (Xavier), the French Battalion moved out at 2000 hours. Effective use of hand grenades and flame throwers reduced the enemy's first resistance, letting First Company come near the first tooth of the hill. Soon Xavier lost more than a section of its troops, and its ammunition ran low. The First Battalion (1/23) resupplied the French company under fire.

The Third Company (Zoé) was then ordered to pass the First to continue the attack even though since the attack on Hill 931 Third Company had been left with only two sections of light infantrymen. Around 2000 hours the lead section of Third Company vaulted over the three hillocks, opening a path as it went with showers of hand grenades.

Huge searchlights positioned on Pia-ri Hill lighted

the battlefield at night. They were so powerful that their beams could illuminate an area almost like daylight. This was achieved in either of two ways: A beam of light could be projected directly onto a hill or ridge to blind the enemy, or the beam could be reflected off some low-lying clouds, thus producing an artificial moon that in turn lighted the ground below.

So rapid had been the advance of the French attackers that they burst right into the middle of the three little hills from both sides, completely taking by surprise the communist defenders, who first looked up from their dug-in positions to see the Frenchmen standing over them like devils in the artificial light. Beyond the three hillocks all was blackness—but standing out in brilliant illumination, was visible the first tooth of Hill 851.

Third Company charged on toward Hill 851 without stopping. Scaling the rocky cleft, the French found most of the holes empty. They killed more than 30 of the enemy and took several prisoners, including three officers. Other of the enemy were seen plunging into the ravines and disappearing into the night.

At 0230 the jubilant Frenchmen were on the hill's crest. Then they realized that they had taken only the first tooth of Hill 851, and that the second tooth still lay 150 meters farther to the north. A broad plateau separated the two teeth.

Meanwhile the Third Battalion (3/23) moved toward 851 from the west, with K Company in the lead. The company, made up of many fresh replacements, moved slowly. The new forward observer had not had time to register artillery before the attack began and found it difficult in the darkness to effect close concentration of the fires with the advancing troops. By 0355 hours a platoon from K Company still had not bridged the gap between its positions and those of the French Battalion.

By early October the folks back home had heard about Heartbreak Ridge and were asking about it. On the 11th Bud Seybert wrote to his family: "You said something about Heartbreak Ridge. Yes, I was there. That is where Al got killed." Bud did not go on to tell his mother and father about all the others that had been killed and wounded on that barren mountain.[12]

On October 12, Seventy-second Tank Battalion ranged deep into enemy territory. They went above Mundung-ni as far north as Hasimpo and westward to within 1,000 meters of Nae-ri. No wonder the Second Division infantrymen called the Seventy-second Tank Battalion their "hidden ball," as in the often-executed football play. This description had proved fully justified.

The drive placed Seventy-second's armor and accompanying infantrymen well behind the North Koreans and newly arrived CCF. At this time, the Second U.S. Infantry Division had the unique distinction of fighting on its front both the North Koreans and the Chinese.

Not to be outdone, Lieutenant Colonel Sturman had driven his tanks well beyond Satae-ri in the eastern valley. With fewer tanks, Task Force Sturman had fully accomplished its mission of softening up the enemy on Hills 656 and 851.

While initially approving General Young's plan to halt the Thirty-eighth Regiment's forward movement and to pull the Ninth Regiment back for training, General Byers, the X Corps commander, now announced a change. He wanted Colonel Mildren's Thirty-eighth to continue northwesterly to seize Hill 1220. To effect this operation, he moved the boundary between the Eighth ROK Division and the Second Infantry Division, placing Hill 1220 (known as Kim Il Sung Range) in Second Division's sector. Instead of going in reserve, the Ninth Regiment would have to take over Thirty-eighth's positions, freeing that regiment for its new mission.

This new plan did not affect the wrap-up of Heartbreak, which was already in its final hours.

That day, October 12, seemed interminably long. The enemy remained solidly entrenched between the French Battalion's positions and those of K Company, which was trying desperately to link up with the French. Every time anyone raised his head just a little, the enemy's machine guns rattled crazily and its mortars thundered, shaking the mountainside.

Friendly mortars and artillery, in turn, rained down upon the enemy and many enemy were killed—to be replaced immediately with fresh Chinese reinforcements. Any renewal of the assault would have to wait for darkness.

At 2100 hours Company A (1/23), reinforced with a section of the French First Company, climbed up the east slopes of 851, but the enemy's automatic weapons, heavy machine guns, and grenade launchers literally stopped the attackers in their tracks.

At 0200 hours the French Second Company moved up to join the rest of the French Battalion. Now all three battalions (1/23, 3/23, and Fr/23) were to attack simultaneously. However, the Twenty-third Regiment gave the French responsibility for directing the artillery fires. The battalion employed a peculiarly French tactic: An artillery barrage fell on 851, shifted to the north, fired deep into the valleys, fired on the enemy's artillery, shifted back to 851, and fired to the left and then to the right. This tactic, which continued until 0400, kept the enemy confused, not knowing where the attackers would direct their effort.

At 0530 elements of the three battalions moved out. First Battalion (1/23) with Company A in the lead advanced successfully. A youthful-appearing sous-lieutenant, Dureau, who had only recently come to Korea straight from Saint-Maxient, led the head platoon of the French Battalion's Second Company. Plunging into a ravine, the men crept along out of sight of the enemy and then climbed up the steep, rocky incline to attack the enemy from the rear. At 0630 hours they found themselves amidst a honeycomb of bunkers.

Dureau had ordered his platoon to fix bayonets. The French bayonet appeared more fierce than the U.S. bayonet, especially in the hands of a Frenchman well-trained in its use. The French either brought with them their own bayonets (which fit perfectly into the

U.S. M-1 rifle) or filed the U.S.-issued bayonet into a sharp, thin, needlelike projection.

After a climactic dash, tossing grenades to block the bunkers' rear exits, and wielding their sharp steel bayonets, the Frenchmen cleared all enemy off 851's summit in several minutes. The prisoners they took, as well as the dead scattered around, were a mixture of North Koreans and Chinese.

K Company, using flame throwers, advanced slowly along the west finger of Hill 851. It met the platoon of Second Company (Yvonne), which descended toward them, knocking out the last enemy bunker along the way. This final link-up at 0730 between the French and Americans secured Hill 851.

Colonel Adams received this message: "We hold it, we keep it. Yvonne has linked up with King. Icicle is on the summit."

Immediately Adams telephoned General Young: "We've got it. We've got it."

His voice breaking, the colonel hung up the phone. Tears streamed down both sides of his face.

"Finally, it is finished!"[13]

Afterword

~~~~~~~~

Thirty-eighth Infantry continued with its mission. The regiment, led by Col. Frank Mildren, assisted by his ever-loyal Executive Officer, Ed Rowney, went on to take Hill 1220 and Kim Il Sung Range. Continuing to speak in terms of football that began with the coinage of Operation Touchdown, General Young, the Second Division Commander, said the Thirty-eighth's seizure of 1220 was "the kick which gave us the point after the touchdown."

Although the Seventy-second Tank Battalion Ninth and Thirty-eighth Regiments took the pressure off the Twenty-third Regiment, assuring its ultimate success, Heartbreak Ridge was from beginning to end the Twenty-third Regiment; and the Twenty-third Regiment was Heartbreak Ridge. And for 30 days, night and day, the whole affair was a heartbreak for the Twenty-third's commander, Col. James Y. Adams.

Second Division was relieved in place by the Seventh Division, the relief taking place from October 21 to October 25. The combat-weary Second Division moved to a quieter sector. Only a few weeks later Colonel Adams received severe injuries from an enemy 120-mm mortar shell. Jim Adams retired from the army in 1961 as a colonel. He now lives in Palo Alto, California, caring for his invalid wife. Adams retrieves abandoned dogs from the pound, and the rescued dogs become his constant companions.

Some of the U.S. survivors of Heartbreak Ridge went to Koje-do to guard the more than 80,000 Chinese and North Korean POWs confined on that island. In the spring, the fanatical communists in the prison camp rioted, and when two of the camp's commanders failed in dealing with the problem, it was Brigadier General Haydon Boatner—The Bull—who was chosen to take charge.

Knowing that his predecessors had gone to Koje-do wearing a brigadier general's one star and had left that infamous place as colonels, Boatner said that he was determined to win at playing the game, "double or nothing."[1] And he did—making use of his extensive knowledge of Asia and his own innate determination.[2]

Wearing two stars, Major General Boatner then took command of the Third Infantry Division at Fort Benning, Georgia, and led that division in one of the last large-scale stateside land maneuvers, Operation

Follow Me. He later became provost marshal of the United States Army.

General Robert Young, also, went to Fort Benning as commandant of the infantry school and took with him as teaching staff Colonel Frank Mildren and other Heartbreak Ridge participants.

Frank Mildren would attain the four stars of a full general and a Vietnam War command. Ed Rowney retired from the army as a major general and in the 1980s held an ambassador's rank, playing a key role in arms control negotiations with the Soviet Union.

General Monclar became Gouverneur des Invalides and died in office in July 1964. Guy de Cockborne and Maurice L. Barthélémy became generals in the French Army. De Cockborne is now mayor of the village of Ervy-le-Chatel, and as president of the Association Nationale des Anciens des Forces Françaises de l'O.N.U. et du Régiment de Corée, participated on October 13, 1984, in dedication of a Paris street named the Place du Battalion Français de l'O.N.U. en Corée 1950–1953. Maj. Serge Bererd served as French-English translator for the occasion.

Lieutenant Dureau, who led the platoon in the final charge on Heartbreak Ridge, now works in the French Import Office in Seoul, Korea. Some of the French Battalion who survived Heartbreak Ridge went to that other Asian war, in Indochina, only to die at Dien Bien Phu.

The U.S. veterans of the Twenty-third Regiment have a unique organization, the Twenty-third Regiment Korean War Branch, that meets annually. Guy Robinson has served as its president.

The Second Division suffered over 3,700 casualties in taking Heartbreak Ridge. This included 597 killed, 3,064 wounded, and 84 missing. Of these casualties, over half (1,832) came from the Twenty-third Regiment and its attached French Battalion.

The North Korean and Chinese losses were even greater. The Second Division estimated the enemy casualties as over 25,000. These included 1,473 counted killed, 8,938 estimated killed, 14,204 estimated wounded, and 606 POWs.[3]

No doubt their decisive defeat at Heartbreak Ridge had something to do with the communists' sudden decision to resume the suspended truce talks. The talks, which had been broken off on August 22, resumed on October 25—less than two weeks after Heartbreak Ridge.

Notes

~~~~~~~~~~

Introduction

1. To this day, official publications of the United States denote it as the Korean "conflict," along with the Vietnam "conflict." All other foreign engagements are called wars. These include the War of 1812 (6,765 casualties), the Mexican War (5,885 casualties), and the Spanish-American War (2,047 casualties). The combined casualties of Korea and Vietnam (337,541) exceed the total U.S. casualties in World War I. The Korean "conflict" casualties alone (136,926) are almost five and one-half times the total of four U.S. wars: Revolutionary, 1812, Mexican, and Spanish-American. The figures cited here are "Battle Deaths"

and "Wounds not Mortal," and do not include "Other Deaths." See *Defense 84: Almanac* (Arlington, Va.: Department of Defense, American Forces Information Service, September 1984).

2. Michael Langley, *Inchon Landing: MacArthur's Last Triumph* (New York: Times Books, 1979).

3. Recent books on the Korean War include J. C. Goulden, *Korea—The Untold Story of the War* (New York: Times Books, 1982); E. P. Hoyt, *The Pusan Perimeter, On to the Yalu,* and *The Bloody Road to Panmunjom* (a trilogy) (New York: Stein & Day, 1984 and 1985); E. Bergot, *Bataillon de Corée: Les Volontaires Français, 1950–1953,* (Paris: France Loisirs, 1983); A. Bevin, *Korea—The First War We Lost* (New York: Hippocrene Books, 1986).

Chapter 1

1. Lt. Col. Le Mire, *L'Assaut de Crevecoeur* (Paris: Aux Carrefours Du Monde 1955).

2. W. G. Hermes, *Truce Tent and Fighting Front* (Washington, D.C.: OCMH, United States Army, 1966), p. 88.

3. Hermes, *Truce Tent,* p. 88, quoting E. C. Williamson, et al., "Action on 'Heartbreak Ridge,'" p. 3, manuscript in OCMH.

4. I have adopted the method of W. G. Hermes in italicizing North Korean and Chinese communist forces unit designations.

5. Le Mire, *L'Assaut de Crevecoeur,* p. 152.

6. John Seybert's letters from Korea to his family, September 1951.

Chapter 2

1. Merle Miller, *Plain Speaking: An Oral Biography of Harry S. Truman* (New York: Greenwich House, 1985), p. 19, quoting Dean Acheson.

2. G. Thomas and M. M. Witts, *Enola Gay* (New York: Stein & Day, 1977), p. 258.

3. M. Truman, *Harry S. Truman* (New York: William Morrow, 1973), p. 1.

4. *Washington Post,* June 24, 1950.

5. Miller, *Plain Speaking,* p. 26.

6. D. Acheson, *The Korean War* (New York: W. W. Norton, 1971), p. 15.

7. *Washington Post,* June 24, 1950.

8. *Independence,* Mo., June 24, 1950.

9. Truman, *Harry S. Truman,* p. 455.

10. Acheson, *Korean War,* p. 25.

11. Ibid. p. 19. To allow this positive U.N. action was surely an incomprehensible bungling by the Soviets. It may be accepted that they had directed the whole scenario for the attack upon South Korea. Possibly their absence from the U.N. at this particular time was preplanned to avoid their being in a position of having to answer accusations of complicity. We will most likely never know what heads may have rolled in the Kremlin for this miscalculation.

12. D. MacArthur, *Reminiscences* (New York: McGraw-Hill, 1964), pp. 332–33.

13. The president very early on June 30, while he was dressing for his morning walk, authorized a regimental combat team to be sent from Japan to Korea. At an 8:30 White House meeting he approved sending two infantry divisions, the Twenty-fourth and Twenty-fifth, from Japan. Acheson, *Korean War,* p. 29. This further action was in response, likewise, to a United Nations call for "members to give Korea such help as might be needed to repel the armed attack and to restore peace in the area." Ibid., p. 23. The resolution, introduced by the United States, was adopted in Joseph Malik's continued absence, with Yugoslavia dissenting and Egypt and India abstaining. Ibid., p. 25.

14. Langley, *Inchon Landing,* p. 8.

15. The defense line ran along the Nakton River north for nearly 100 miles and then east 50 miles to Yongdok on the Sea of Japan. J. F. Schnebel, *Policy and Direction: The First Year* (Washington, D.C.: OCMH, United States Army, 1972), p. 127.

16. Langley, *Inchon Landing,* p. 17.

17. Ibid.

18. Ibid.

19. Schnebel, *Policy and Direction,* p. 152.

20. Ibid., p. 177.

21. Ibid., p. 275.

22. Langley, *Inchon Landing,* p. 21.

23. M. B. Ridgway, *The Korean War* (New York: Doubleday, 1967), p. 81.

24. This defense line extended from Pyongtack on the west coast eastward through Wonchon in the

center to Samchok on the east coast. Schnebel, *Policy and Direction,* p. 309, and Map VIII.

25. Ibid., p. 363 and Map IX.

26. Ibid., p. 380.

27. Ibid., p. 389.

28. Ibid., p. 398.

29. Ibid and Map IX.

Chapter 3

1. Le Mire, *L'Assaut de Crevecoeur,* p. 157.

2. Hermes, *Truce Tent,* p. 81.

3. Ibid., p. 86.

4. J. Toland, *Battle: The Story of the Bulge* (New York: Random House, 1959), p. 180ff.

5. Gen. Frank T. Mildren, interview with author, September 1984.

6. W. G. Hermes, *Truce Tent,* p. 88.

7. Major General Ruffner, Second Division commander, had returned home on normal rotation on September 1 but his replacement had not yet arrived.

8. Command Reports, Second Infantry Division, September 1951. (Hereafter cited Cmd. Rpts., Sept. 1951.)

9. Cmd. Rpts., Sept. 1951.

10. Ibid.

11. Guy Robinson, interview with author, April 1985.

12. Albert Terney, interview with author, January 1985.

13. Cmd. Rpts., Sept. 1951.

14. Ibid.

15. Ibid.

16. James Y. Adams, interview with author, July 1985.

17. Cmd. Rpts., Sept. 1951.

18. Ibid.

19. Ibid.

20. Sergeant Hall received the Silver Star (1st OLC), GO 656, Second Infantry Division, October 31, 1951.

21. Cmd. Rpts., Sept. 1951.

22. Col. Louis-Christian Michelet, interview with author, Paris, October 1984.

Chapter 4

1. Le Mire, *L'Assaut de Crevecoeur,* p. 164.

2. Charles Rothenberg, interview with author, July 1985.

3. Carl Kleinpeter, interview with author, July 1984; Olen Kleinpeter, interview with author, July 1985.

4. Maj. Gen. Richard Kotite, interview with author, September 1985.

5. Lt. Daniel Williams, interview with author, September 1984.

6. Lt. Col. James Dick, interview with author, July 1985.

7. Ibid.

Chapter 5

1. Robinson interview.

2. Le Mire, *L'Assaut de Crevecoeur,* p. 168.

3. Maj. Gen. Emory S. Adams was the adjutant general, United States Army, from 1938 to 1942.

4. Clay Blair, *Ridgway's Paratroopers: The American Airborne in World War II* (Garden City, N.J.: Dial Press, Doubleday, 1985), p. 57.

5. Cmd. Rpts., Sept. 1951.

6. Adams interview.

7. Dick interview.

8. Gaither Nicholas, interview with author, July 1985.

9. Le Mire, *L'Assaut de Crevecoeur,* pp. 164–65.

10. Lt. C. C. Munroe, *The Second United States Infantry Division in Korea, 1950–1951* (Tokyo: Toppan Printing Co. n.d.), p. 173.

11. B. W. Tuchman, *Stilwell and the American Experience in China, 1911–45* (New York: Macmillan, 1971), pp. 430–31.

12. Maj. Gen. Haydon L. Boatner, as stated to the author, 1954.

13. Joe Melton, interview with author, October 1984.

Chapter 6

1. Le Mire, *L'Assaut de Crevecoeur,* p. 194.

2. This well-known quotation was said, not by General Pershing, but by one of his staff officers.

3. H. Feis, *Japan Subdued* (Princeton, N.J.: Princeton University Press, 1961), p. 82, note 55.

4. Acheson, *Korean War*, p. 23.

5. In the French Army a general officer equivalent to a U.S. lieutenant general wears four stars.

6. Guy de Cockborne's ancestor, Adam de Cockburn, had come from Scotland to France in 1578 to marry Gabrielle de Fontaines, dame de Villeneuve-au-Chemin.

7. Michelet interview.

8. Le Mire, *L'Assaut de Crevecoeur,* p. 158.

9. Correspondence from Lt. Col. James Dick to the author, November 27, 1984.

10. Le Mire, *L'Assaut de Crevecoeur,* p. 166.

11. Ibid.

Chapter 7

1. This account of the meeting between General Monclar, Major Le Mire, and Colonel Adams is taken from Le Mire, *L'Assaut de Crevecoeur,* p. 168.

2. M. B. Ridgway, *The Korean War* (New York: Doubleday, 1967), p. 189.

3. Supporting Documents ("Briefing Notes"), Second Infantry Division, October 1951, pp. 2–3. (Hereafter cited Spt. Doc.)

4. Corporal Harsh was awarded the Bronze Star, GO 28, Second Infantry Division, January 1, 1952.

5. Captain Daniels received the Silver Star, GO 24, Second Infantry Division, January 18, 1952.

6. Lt. J. Boynton, "The Satae-ri Valley, Korea—1951, *Mustang News,* summer 1984.

7. Maj. Serge Bererd, interview with author, Paris, October 1984.

8. Lt. Col. V. E. "Operation Touchdown Won Heartbreak Ridge," *Combat Forces Journal* (December 1953), p. 28.

9. Command Report, Second Infantry Division, October 1951. (Hereafter cited Cmd. Rpts., Oct. 1951.)

Chapter 8

1. Craven, *Operation Touchdown,* p. 25.

2. Heartbreak Crossroads was the name given to Wahlerscheid Crossroads in Belgium; see Toland, *Battle,* p. 68.

3. Ibid., p. 69.

4. Cmd. Rpts., Oct. 1951.

5. Craven, *Operation Touchdown,* pp. 27–28.

6. Private First Class Underwood received the Silver Star, GO 15, Second Infantry Division, January 13, 1952.

7. Craven, *Operation Touchdown,* p. 28.

8. Cmd. Rpts., Oct. 1951.

9. Amb. Edward Rowney, interview with author, September 1984.

10. Cmd. Rpts., Oct. 1951.

11. Spt. Doc., p. 7.

12. Sergeant First Class Rhea was awarded the

Silver Star, GO 29, Second Infantry Division, January 1, 1952.

13. Private Beach was posthumously awarded the Silver Star, GO 12, Second Infantry Division, January 1, 1952.

14. Lt. Col. Eugene Craven, interview with author, August 1984.

15. Spt. Doc., p. 7.

16. Private First Class Willis received the Bronze Star, GO 735, Second Infantry Division, November 18, 1951.

17. Private Cotta was awarded the Bronze Star, GO 735, Second Infantry Division, November 18, 1951.

18. Corporal Burtness was awarded the Silver Star, GO 740, Second Infantry Division, November 19, 1951.

19. Cmd. Rpts., Oct. 1951.

20. Rowney interview.

21. Spt. Doc., p. 9.

22. Cmd. Rpts., Oct. 1951.

23. Corporal Bartley received the Bronze Star, GO 735, Second Infantry Division, November 18, 1951.

Chapter 9

1. Capt. S. Freedman, "Tankers at Heartbreak," *Armor* (September–October 1952), p. 24.

2. Cmd. Rpts.

3. Craven, *Operation Touchdown*, p. 29.

4. Freedman, *Tankers*, p. 25.

5. Cmd. Rpts.

6. Corporal Vaughan's actions won him the Silver Star, GO 74, Second Infantry Division, January 30, 1952.

7. Private First Class Sullivan received the Silver Star, GO 37, Second Infantry Division, January 23, 1952.

8. The taking of Hill 520 is covered in detail in Capt. R. A. Gugelar, *Combat Actions in Korea: Infantry, Artillery, Armor* (Washington, D.C.: Combat Forces Press, 1954). That book details several small-unit actions, carefully selected primarily for the teaching of junior officers, noncommissioned officers, and privates. Although Chapter 18 in his book is entitled "Heartbreak Ridge," the introductory paragraph clearly points out that Hill 520 was only a "small subsidiary portion—a hump at the western end of a spur from the Heartbreak ridgeline."

Unfortunately, subsequent authors have included the Hill 520 action under the chapter headings "Heartbreak Ridge" in a manner that might lead the reader to believe that it was the main action of that noted battle. In G. Forty, *At War in Korea* (Shepperton: Ian Allan, 1982), the Gugelar account is quoted verbatim and credit is given to that author; but in E. P. Hoyt, *The Bloody Road to Panmunjom* (New York: Stein & Day, 1985), the Gugelar story is paraphrased in the chapter "Heartbreak Ridge." There is no indication of the relative importance of Hill 520 to the larger battle except to state that most of the ridgeline had fallen into U.N. hands, leaving this one small eminence. No reference to the original author nor to his purpose in detailing the Hill 520 action is apparent.

9. Le Mire, *L'Assaut de Crevecoeur,* pp. 173–74.

10. Ibid., p. 172.

11. Sergeant Rakowiecki received the Silver Star, GO 33 Second Infantry Division, January 21, 1952.

12. John Seybert's letter to his family, October 11, 1951.

13. Le Mire, *L'Assaut de Crevecoeur,* p. 179.

Afterword

1. Major General Boatner, as told to the author, 1954.

2. T. R. Fehrenback, *This Kind of War* (New York: MacMillan, 1963), pp. 575–94.

3. Hermes, *Truce Tent,* p. 96.

Bibliography

~~~~~~~~~~

Books

Acheson, Dean. *The Korean War*. New York: W. W. Norton & Co., 1971.

Bevin, A. *Korea—The First War We Lost*. New York: Hippocrene Books, 1986.

Blair, Clay. *Ridgway's Paratroopers: The American Airborne in World War II*. Garden City, NY: Doubleday, 1985.

Fehrenback, T. R. *This Kind of War*. New York: MacMillan, 1963.

Feis, H. *Japan Subdued*. Princeton, NJ: Princeton University Press, 1961.

Forty, G. *At War in Korea.* Shepperton, Surrey, England: Ian Allan, 1982.

Goulden, J. C. *Korea—The Untold Story of the War.* New York: Times Books, 1982.

Gugeler, R. A. *Combat Action in Korea: Infantry, Artillery, Armor.* Washington, D.C.: Combat Forces Press, 1954.

Hermes, W. G. *Truce Tent and Fighting Front.* Washington, D.C.: OCMH, United States Army, 1966.

Hoyt, E. P. *The Pusan Perimeter, On to the Yalu,* and *The Bloody Road to Panmunjom* (a trilogy). New York: Stein & Day, 1984 and 1985.

Langley, Michael. *Inchon Landing: MacArthur's Last Triumph.* New York: Times Books, 1979.

Le Mire, Oliver, Lt. Col. *L'Assaut de Crevecoeur.* Paris: Aux Carrefours Du Monde, 1955.

MacArthur, D. *Reminiscences.* New York: MacGraw-Hill Co., 1964.

Miller, Merle. *Plain Speaking: An Oral Biography of Harry S. Truman.* New York: Greenwich House, 1985.

Munroe, C. C., Lt. *The United States Second Infantry Division in Korea, 1950–1951.* Tokyo: n.d. Toppan Printing Co.

Ridgway, M. B. *The Korean War.* New York: Doubleday, 1967.

Schnebel, J. F. *Policy and Direction: The First Year.* Washington, D.C.: OCMH, United States Army, 1972.

Thomas, G., & Witts, M. M. *Enola Gay.* New York: Stein & Day, 1971.

Bibliography

Toland, J. *Battle: The Story of the Bulge.* New York: Random House, 1959.

Truman, M. *Harry S. Truman.* New York: William Morrow, 1973.

Tuchman, B. W. *Stilwell and the American Experience in China 1911–45.* New York: Macmillan, 1971.

Articles

Boynton, J., Lt. "The Satae-ri Valley, Korea—1951," *Mustang News,* summer 1984.

Craven, V. E., Lt. Col. "Operation Touchdown Won Heartbreak Ridge" *Combat Forces Journal* December 1953.

Freedman, S., Capt. "Tankers at Heartbreak," *Armor,* September-October 1952.

Archives and Manuscript Collections

Cas Concret No. 3. Crevecoeur (supplied by Jean-Louis Posiere, Maromme, France).

Command Reports, Second United States Army Infantry Division, September-October 1951, United States Archives, Suitland, Md.

Command Reports, Ninth, Twenty-third, and Thirty-eighth Infantry Regiments, Second United States Army Infantry Division. September-October 1951, United States Archives, Suitland, Md.

De l'Organisation, des Nations Unies. French Embassy, Washington, D.C.

Bibliography

Diary. Dick, James, Capt. 1951.

Diary. Myers, Raymond, Pfc. 1951.

General Orders, Second United States Army Infantry
Division. September 1951–January 1952, U.S.
Archives, Suitland, Md.

Private Collection, Korean War. De Cockborne, General. Ervy-Le-Chatel, France.

Name and Subject Index

Index

Index

Index

U.S. Army Index

Index

About the Author

ARNED LEE HINSHAW, a physician and an attorney, has pursued alternately civilian and military careers. His military career, from which he retired in 1986 as a Colonel, United States Army, spanned 41 years of both active and reserve service. He is a graduate of the Infantry School, Fort Benning, Georgia, and of the Command and General Staff College, Fort Leavenworth, Kansas. His academic degrees include a B.A. and a J.D. from the University of North Carolina at Chapel Hill and an M.D. from Duke University. He lives in Durham, North Carolina, with his wife, Virginia.

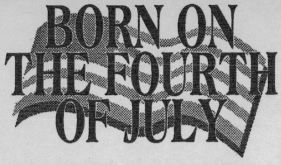

BORN ON THE FOURTH OF JULY

RON KOVIC

A true story of innocence lost and courage found.

He was a natural athlete, a shy teenager, an All American working-class kid. He shipped out to Vietnam with the Marines. Ron Kovic didn't come marching home. He was wounded, paralyzed permanently from the chest down.

This is Ron Kovic's story - a searing, graphic, deeply moving account of a young man whose real war began in the devastating aftermath of Vietnam.

☐ **BORN ON THE FOURTH OF JULY**
68149/$4.50

POCKET
B O O K S